Healthcare Antitrust FAQ Handbook

First Edition

Authors:

Mark L. Mattioli, Esquire, Project Chair

Alexander M. McIntyre, Jr., Esquire

Stephen P. Murphy, Esquire

David M. Narrow, Esquire

Patricia M. Wagner, Esquire

Hillary A. Webber, Esquire

AMERICAN
HEALTH LAWYERS
ASSOCIATION

*"This publication is designed to provide accurate and authoritative information
with respect to the subject matter covered. It is provided with the understanding
that the publisher is not engaged in rendering legal or other professional services.
If legal advice or other expert assistance is required, the services of a competent
professional person should be sought."*
— from a declaration of the American Bar Association

RECENT TITLES FROM HEALTH LAWYERS

False Claims Act & The Healthcare Industry: Counseling & Litigation,
Second Edition with 2012 Cumulative Supplement
© 2012, perfect bound

Legal Issues in Healthcare Fraud and Abuse: Navigating the Uncertainties, Fourth Edition
© 2012, perfect bound

The ACO Handbook: A Guide to Accountable Care Organizations,
First Edition with CD-ROM
© 2012, perfect bound

AHLA's Federal Healthcare Laws & Regulations, 2011-2012 Edition with CD-ROM
© 2011, perfect bound

Health Plans Contracting Handbook, Sixth Edition with CD-ROM,
© 2011, perfect bound

AHLA's Guide to Healthcare Legal Forms, Agreements, and Policies,
First Edition with November 2011 Supplement and CD-ROM
© 2011, loose leaf

Healthcare Finance, Second Edition with CD-ROM
© 2011, perfect bound

Data Breach Notification Laws : A Fifty State Survey with Federal Breach Notification
Research Guide , First Edition (no CD)
© 2011, perfect bound

The Medical & Healthcare Facility Lease: Legal and Business Handbook,
First Edition with CD-ROM
© 2011, perfect bound

Healthcare Compliance Legal Issues Manual, Third Edition with CD-ROM
© 2011, perfect bound

Healthcare Entity Bylaws and Related Documents: Navigating
the Medical Staff/Healthcare Entity Relationship, Third Edition with CD-ROM
© 2011, perfect bound

Fundamentals of Health Law, Fifth Edition with CD-ROM
© 2011, perfect bound

The Law of Health Information Technology, First Edition with CD-ROM
© 2011, perfect bound

AHLA's Guide to Healthcare Legal Forms, Agreements, and Policies, First Edition
with November 2010 Supplement with CD-ROM
© 2010, loose leaf

Physician Recruitment and Compensation Arrangements Practice Guide,
Third Edition with CD-ROM
© 2010, perfect bound

AHLA Federal Healthcare Laws & Regulations, August 2010 Healthcare Reform Update
to 2009-2010 Edition with CD-ROM
© 2010, perfect bound

Institutional Review Boards: A Primer, Second Edition with CD-ROM
© 2010, perfect bound

Deciphering Codes: Fraud & Abuse for Coders and Coding Insight
for Healthcare Lawyers, First Edition with CD-ROM
© 2010, loose leaf

Peer Review Guidebook, Fourth Edition with CD-ROM
© 2010, perfect bound

Peer Review Hearing Guidebook, First Edition with CD-ROM
© 2010, perfect bound

Preface

In March 2012, the Federal Trade Commission (FTC) ordered two hospitals to unwind the merger that they had previously agreed to, and a month later in April a United States District Court temporarily blocked the merger of two hospitals pending FTC administrative proceedings challenging the merger. These are two recent examples of how antitrust laws can affect business deals in the healthcare industry. Whether you are in-house counsel with a healthcare organization, a healthcare attorney not generally involved with antitrust issues, or even one more familiar with how antitrust issues impact healthcare organizations, you will benefit from this handy guide to what is and isn't allowed in the healthcare antitrust context.

Health Lawyers is pleased to bring you the *Healthcare Antitrust FAQ Handbook, First Edition*. We greatly appreciate the work by authors Mark L. Mattioli, Esquire, Alexander M. McIntyre, Jr., Esquire, David M. Narrow, Esquire, Stephen P. Murphy, Esquire, Patricia M. Wagner, Esquire, and Hillary A. Webber, Esquire, as well as the numerous editors for their work on this important project.

This *Handbook* is set up as a series of questions that will allow one to begin to understand the antitrust implications that will be critical to structuring deals for your clients. The subjects covered include not only the traditional antitrust questions affecting mergers and acquisitions, competition, and the Robinson-Patman Antidiscrimination Act (Robinson-Patman), but other subjects specific to healthcare such as the antitrust implications in the peer review and medical staff arena, physician and other healthcare provider networks, and sharing healthcare price information.

Questions include when it is permissible to talk to a competitor about merging and what information can be shared, how do federal antitrust agencies determine when to challenge mergers, how can you take advantage of the immunity protection of the Health Care Quality Improvement Act of 1986 (HCQIA) in credentialing matters, when are exclusive contracts with primary payers permissible, what type of provider network arrangements can avoid *per se* condemnation, and what authority do state attorneys general have to investigate federal antitrust violations? In addition, the questions and answers are bolstered by extensive footnotes to aid the reader in further expanding their research into each area of coverage.

Health Lawyers commends the *Healthcare Antitrust FAQ Handbook* to all health law attorneys, who need to understand the intricacies of adhering to the laws and regulations enacted to promote competition in healthcare. We anticipate that the *Handbook* will prove to be a useful guide for attorneys, compliance officers and their clients in understanding this area of the law.

About the Editors

David A. Argue, Ph.D., is a Principal at Economists Incorporated in its Washington, DC, office. He has taught health economics courses at Johns Hopkins University. Dr. Argue received his Ph.D. in economics from the University of Virginia in 1990. He has analyzed competition and performed damages analyses in various healthcare markets for government investigations and private antitrust litigation. Among the healthcare areas in which Dr. Argue has worked are hospitals, physician practices, ambulatory surgery centers, health insurance, and pharmaceuticals. He has performed damages analyses related to alleged harm to competition among healthcare providers and payers, disputes related to alleged restrictive payer-provider contracts, loss of income from termination of physicians' privileges, and in other areas. He has written and spoken on healthcare matters numerous times over the past 20 years.

Saralisa C. Brau, Esquire, is a Deputy Assistant Director in the Health Care Division of the Federal Trade Commission's Bureau of Competition in Washington, DC. Saralisa leads investigations and litigation involving alleged violations of the antitrust laws by pharmaceutical companies, physicians, hospitals, and other healthcare providers. Saralisa joined the FTC in 2005. Prior to that, Saralisa was with the law firm of McDermott Will & Emery in New York, NY, where her practice focused on antitrust counseling, antitrust civil litigation, and trade regulation matters, often for healthcare industry clients. Saralisa regularly represented clients before the FTC and Department of Justice in antitrust conduct, merger, and criminal investigations. She is a graduate of the University of Virginia School of Law, and holds a Bachelor of Arts degree, cum laude, from Duke University.

Christi J. Braun, Esquire, is a Partner in Mintz Levin's Antitrust and Health Law Sections. She focuses on litigation of antitrust and commercial matters and counsels doctors, hospitals, insurance companies, and pharmaceutical companies on issues involving antitrust compliance, mergers and acquisitions, and joint-ventures. Prior to private practice, Ms. Braun served as a staff attorney in the Health Care Services & Products Division of the Federal Trade Commission. She is admitted to practice in the District of Columbia, New York, and Colorado, as well as before the United States Supreme Court. Ms. Braun was listed as a 2009 Outstanding Healthcare Antitrust Lawyer in *Nightingale's Healthcare News*.

Ralph Breitfeller, Esquire, is Of Counsel to Kegler, Brown, Hill & Ritter, in Columbus, OH, where he practices primarily in the areas of healthcare and antitrust law. He represents healthcare providers including physicians, pharmacies, drug distributors, drug repackagers, home health agencies, and durable medical equipment suppliers. He advises healthcare providers on the regulatory aspects of mergers and acquisitions. In the course of his antitrust practice, he advises clients on distribution arrangements, pricing, and Hart-Scott-Rodino premerger notification. He also represents clients in antitrust litigation.

Mark L. Mattioli, Esquire (Project Chair and author of the Introduction and Chapter 2, Medical Staff and Peer Review), of Marshall Dennehey Warner Coleman & Goggin PC, focuses his litigation and consulting practice on solving complex business problems in a variety of highly regulated areas. He directs his extensive litigation and consulting experience to the representation of clients in the healthcare, financial, and insurance industries, where he has handled numerous complex commercial litigation and class action matters involving antitrust, Medicare fraud, copyright and trademark infringement, tortious interference, breach of contract, civil rights, employment, debt collection, negligence, and strict liability-based claims. He has represented numerous professionals in disciplinary disputes where they have been faced with the loss of their livelihoods and has extensive experience in the area of electronic discovery, especially as it relates to the healthcare industry. Mr. Mattioli routinely counsels hospitals and health systems regarding antitrust compliance, general commercial matters, and other issues related to the credentialing of practitioners. He recently served as Vice Chair for the Antitrust Practice Group of the American Health Lawyers Association. Mr. Mattioli has litigated cases nationally and has written extensively on the topics of antitrust, fraud and abuse, medical staff credentialing, and aviation law.

Joseph M. Miller, Esquire, is the General Counsel of American Health Insurance Plans (AHIP). Prior to joining AHIP he served in the Antitrust Division of the Department of Justice (DOJ) from 1998 until 2010, including six years as the Assistant Chief of the Litigation I Section. There, he oversaw enforcement and competition advocacy in a wide variety of industries, including healthcare and insurance markets. Before joining the DOJ, Mr. Miller worked for Collier, Shannon, Rill & Scott and as a trial attorney for the Federal Trade Commission. He is a 1991 graduate of the George Mason University School of Law and earned an undergraduate degree in economics from Emory University in 1986.

About the Authors

Alexander M. McIntyre, Jr., Esquire (author of Chapters 1, Mergers, Joint Ventures, and Affiliations, and 3, Healthcare Competition Issues), is Of Counsel to Baker, Donelson, Bearman, Caldwell & Berkowitz, based in its New Orleans office. Mr. McIntyre's practice focuses on antitrust and trade regulation matters, with an emphasis on healthcare antitrust matters, such as hospital mergers, physician networks, obtaining Certificates of Public Advantage for healthcare transactions, and other provider joint ventures. He has represented healthcare clients before state and federal agencies, as well as in state and federal courts, and is the Chair of the Antitrust and Trade Regulation Section of the Louisiana State Bar Association.

Stephen P. Murphy, Esquire (Chapter 5, The Robinson-Patman Act, and Chapter 7, Price and Nonprice Information and Group Purchasing), is a partner in the Antitrust/Competition Practice Group at Edwards Wildman Palmer LLP in its Washington, DC, office. Mr. Murphy's practice focuses on advising clients in the healthcare and pharmaceutical sectors on pricing and distribution issues. In addition, he has represented clients before the Department of Justice, the Federal Trade Commission, and State Attorneys' General on issues related to investigations of cartel conduct in healthcare and other fields. Mr. Murphy has successfully and effectively litigated antitrust cases in trial and appellate courts all over the country. He provides antitrust advice to clients engaged in mergers, investments, and acquisitions. Mr. Murphy is a contributing author to the recently published ABA Section of Antitrust Law, Antitrust Law Developments (7th ed. 2012).

David M. Narrow, Esquire (Chapter 4, Physicians and Other Healthcare Provider Networks), is recently retired from the Health Care Division of the Federal Trade Commission's Bureau of Competition, after nearly 35 years of service there. Most recently, Mr. Narrow headed up the Health Care Division's advisory opinion program and was the principal drafter of most of that office's advisory opinions regarding clinical integration and provider networks, as well as advisory opinions on a variety of other issues. He drafted the document "Guidance from Staff of the Bureau of Competition's Health Care Division on Requesting and Obtaining an Advisory Opinion" (available on the FTC's website). Mr. Narrow participated in the development and drafting of the 1993, 1994, and 1996 joint FTC/Department of Justice Statements of Antitrust Enforcement Policy in Health Care, contributed to the recently adopted FTC/DOJ Statement of Antitrust Enforcement Policy Regarding Accountable Care Organizations Participating in the Medicare Shared Savings Program (Oct. 2011), and contributed to the joint FTC/DOJ report: "Improving Health Care: A Dose of Competition" (July 2004). He has participated in numerous antitrust investigations and litigation efforts involving alleged anticompetitive activity in healthcare delivery and financing markets, hospital, hospital system, and other healthcare organization mergers, and pharmaceutical "pay-for-delay" cases. Mr. Narrow has participated in numerous FTC interventions and presentations, including agency testimony, policy papers, written comments, and oral presentations before congressional committees and committee staff, state agencies, and international competition/antitrust delegations and organizations. He has participated in the preparation of appellate court briefs in several FTC healthcare matters. He also has spoken before numerous healthcare industry, antitrust bar, and government law enforcement groups and organizations. In addition to his law degree, Mr. Narrow holds an M.P.H. degree.

Leia C. Olsen, Esquire (contributing author to Chapter 4), is an associate in the Milwaukee, WI, office of Hall, Render, Killian, Heath & Lyman, P.C. Ms. Olsen's health law practice focuses on regulatory compliance, billing and reimbursement, patient privacy, and antitrust. Her practice includes helping clients conduct internal investigations, preparing self-disclosures and responding to federal investigations, providing guidance on Medicare and Medicaid billing and payment issues, and advising clients on financial arrangements between hospitals and physicians.

Patricia M. Wagner, Esquire (Chapter 6, Healthcare Payer Issues), is a member of the firm of Epstein Becker & Green PC. Ms. Wagner represents a wide range of healthcare clients in all aspects of antitrust counseling and has worked with clients to develop general strategies to achieve corporate antitrust compliance in all aspects of their business processes, including advising clients on antitrust issues that arise in contracting or other business ventures, and assisting clients in developing protocols to foster antitrust compliance. Ms. Wagner regularly represents clients in front of the Federal Trade Commission and the Department of Justice. She recently participated on a panel hosted by the FTC related to the FTC/DOJ Proposed Statement on antitrust compliance for Accountable Care Organizations participating in the Medicare Shared Savings Program.

Hillary A. Webber, Esquire (Chapter 8, Litigation and Enforcement), is an associate in the Antitrust and Competition group at McDermott Will & Emery LLP. She focuses her practice on antitrust litigation, civil and criminal antitrust government investigations, and defense of mergers and acquisitions before the U.S. antitrust agencies. Ms. Webber has particular experience in healthcare antitrust and frequently advises clients on issues such as clinical integration and potential acquisitions among physician groups and hospitals. She has successfully navigated managed care and life sciences clients through the merger review process and conduct investigations.

Introduction

Mark L. Mattioli, Esquire
Marshall Dennehey Warner Coleman & Goggin PC

This book is the product of interaction of the various practice groups of the American Health Lawyers Association. It represents some of the issues that the Antitrust Practice Group is frequently asked to address by other practice groups. The authors' purpose is not to provide a lengthy discourse of antitrust law with extensive citations or provide the seasoned antitrust practitioner with a guide to draft an appellate brief or respond to an investigation initiated by the Federal Trade Commission, Department of Justice Antitrust Division, or State Attorneys' General Office.

Rather, this is a practical book directed at corporate counsel, general healthcare practitioners, and antitrust practitioners who are looking for short, accurate, and concise presentations of typical antitrust questions that are raised in the healthcare context. The purpose is to provide a summary of antitrust issues present in a particular context and, more important, to provide the necessary information to determine whether additional research is necessary. For corporate counsel, given the multitude of roles and legal disciplines often encountered, this book will provide guidance to determine whether additional assistance is needed from antitrust counsel, and if so, provide corporate counsel with a basic understanding of an issue so that counsel can confidently discuss the work that needs to be done by outside counsel.

For the general healthcare practitioner, it will provide guidance on a particular situation's possible antitrust risks and provide a starting point for additional research. Finally, for the seasoned antitrust practitioner, it provides an easy-to-use reference, especially for areas where the practitioner may be less versed and needs a brief refresher and citations to the primary authorities for further research.

The book is set up as a series of questions that may be considered as an index to assist you in finding the relevant materials. Some of the discussions are lengthy because the questions are more vague and involve more complex answers. It goes without saying that the answers are general, and because antitrust analysis is often based on specific factual circumstances, no answer should be deemed definitive for a particular situation at hand.

The user is not required to read each chapter in its entirety, as the core issues that are involved with each question are presented within the confines of the specific question. However, as there is overlap, it may be helpful to review similar questions to better understand the concepts.

The book assumes some basic knowledge of antitrust, such as the basic elements of the Sherman Antitrust Act, and does not purport to be an elementary treatise.

Table of Contents

1

Mergers, Joint Ventures, and Affiliations

Alexander M. McIntyre, Jr., Esquire

Baker, Donelson, Bearman, Caldwell & Berkowitz PC

A primary function of the antitrust enforcement agencies is to evaluate mergers' competitive effects. At the federal level, this task is shared by the Department of Justice (DOJ) and the Federal Trade Commission (FTC). The central issue in this type of review is whether the transaction will create or enhance a firm's ability to exercise market power in the relevant market. Often, this is through a price increase that can be forced on unwilling consumers and buyers of services. This chapter discusses the way the federal agencies analyze proposed mergers and issues the parties need to consider when discussing a merger or substantial transaction. In addition, the chapter looks at the concept of the virtual merger and retrospective challenges to already consummated mergers.

1.1 A COMPETITOR CALLED AND WANTS TO TALK ABOUT A MERGER OR OTHER AFFILIATION. IS IT POSSIBLE TO MEET WITH THE COMPETITOR? WHAT CAN BE DISCUSSED?

Yes, it is possible to meet with a competitor to discuss an affiliation, what can be done together, and how it might be accomplished. However, there are constraints on what can be discussed and how to begin to implement any arrangement. Also, as a rule, matters of common concern to the industry and publically available information can be discussed. At this point in the process, it is not appropriate to discuss (except in the most general way) individual price, cost, reimbursement rates, specific salaries, particular customers or suppliers, or other competitively sensitive information. A good, if obvious, rule of thumb is that if the company or company's representative considers a topic or information to be confidential, it probably should not be discussed with a competitor.

More particularly with regard to discussing a possible merger, joint venture, or other affiliation, it is appropriate to talk about publically known business conditions, events, or industry or community needs and wants. For example, in a particular community, it may be well known that the healthcare industry as a whole, and certain major institutional providers in particular, are suffering economically. In such circumstances, discussions among competitors concerning efficiencies and cost savings achievable by collaboration should be encouraged. However, there should be no informal discussions or agreement on prices, rates, utilization, or costs. For example, the discussion of potential joint purchasing arrangements between two hospitals is unlikely to be improper especially if the hospitals together would not have significant power in the market for purchasing particular goods. An agreement between two hospitals that one will stop using its magnetic resonance imaging machine if the other will stop performing computed tomography scans, however, is probably not appropriate.

It is important to know that the DOJ and the FTC have jointly promulgated certain guidelines on cooperation among competitors. These guidelines, obtainable on the agencies' Web sites, range from the more general *Guidelines for Collaborations Among Competitors* and *Horizontal Merger Guidelines*, to the more industry specific, such as the agencies' *Statements of Antitrust Enforcement Policy in Health Care*. The latter are particularly helpful, including guidelines and safe harbors regarding hospital mergers, hospital joint ventures involving particularly expensive medical equipment or specialized or expensive clinical services, information exchange, and joint purchasing arrangements. These guidelines are helpful in identifying acceptable discussions among competitors. In the example above, a joint purchasing arrangement between two small hospitals or clinics is likely to fall within an antitrust safety zone; therefore, preliminary discussions concerning such collaboration will be proper. However, a merger between the only two cardiology practices in a particular city would probably not withstand the agencies' scrutiny, so any discussion of such a merger is automatically suspect.

More generally, in any contact with competitors it is important to remember that price-fixing is a *per se* violation of the Sherman Act and may be subject to criminal prosecution. Importantly, too, illegal price-fixing can constitute more than just agreeing with a competitor on the price at which each will sell his product. Among agreements found to be illegal are those concerning: credit terms;[1] limiting discounts;[2] discounting free services;[3] use of

---

[1] *See, e.g.,* Catalano, Inc. v. Target Sales, 446 U.S. 643 (per curiam).

[2] *See, e.g.,* United States v. Stop & Shop Cos., 1984 WL 3196 (D.Conn.).

[3] *See, e.g.,* United States v. Aquafredda, 834 F.2d 915 (11th Cir. 1987).

a common sales agent to fix prices;[4] prohibiting premiums;[5] and restricting advertising.[6] Accordingly, *any* mention of *anything* concerning price is suspect (except in the broadest generalizations possible).

The following is an example of a "Do" and "Don't" checklist.

DO'S

- **DO** consult with the legal department on all antitrust questions that may arise.

- **DO** protect against any discussions or activities that appear to violate this checklist; disassociate yourself from any such discussions or activities and leave any setting in which they continue.

- **DO** engage in "smart writing" and consider not only what you intend to say in a written document (e.g., e-mail), but also how you say it and how those reading it may interpret or possibly misinterpret it.

- **DO** share drafts of Term Sheets, memoranda of understanding, proposed business plans, etc., with the legal department.

- **DO** write down the legitimate business reasons for proposed actions/ mergers and acquisitions/joint ventures/alliances and the 'competitive benefits of any proposed strategy.

DON'TS

- **DO NOT** discuss or exchange, with actual or prospective competitors, whether in public or private, in a business or social setting, in seriousness or jest, information regarding:

    - Company prices, price changes, price differentials, markups, discounts, allowances, terms of sale, or credit terms;

    - Company figures on costs, wages/benefits, production, backlog, capacity, inventories, or sales;

    - Industry pricing policies, price levels, price changes, or differentials;

    - Changes in industry production, capacity, or inventories;

    - Future business plans;

    - Specific customers;

---

[4] *See, e.g.,* Citizen Public, Co. v. United States, 394 U.S. 131 (1969).

[5] *See, e.g.,* United States v. Gasoline Retailers Ass'n, 285 F.2d 688 (7th Cir. 1961).

[6] *See, e.g.,* Blackburn v. Sweeney, 53 F.3d 825 (7th Cir. 1995.) (A more complete list of agreements found to constitute illegal price-fixing is available at "Antitrust Law Developments" (6th ed. 2007) *ABA Section of Antitrust Law,* at pp. 81–90.)

- Company plans concerning the design, production, distribution, or marketing of particular products or services, including proposed territories or customers;

- Matters relating to actual or potential customers or suppliers that might have the effect of excluding them from any market or of influencing the business conduct of firms toward each other's customers or suppliers.

- **DO NOT** make statements that a particular customer, contract, or sale territory "belongs" to a certain company.

- **DO NOT** target or gang up on specific competitors.

- **DO NOT** urge, incite, or signal competitors not to deal with a buyer or seller (as in a boycott).

- **DO NOT** engage in illegal or clandestine actions to obtain competitive data.

- **DO NOT** accept or use competitive data disclosed in breach of a confidentiality obligation.

- **DO NOT** disclose or use competitive data marked "confidential" without first contacting the legal department.

- **DO NOT** make untrue, unfounded, or misleading statements about competitors' products or services or make untrue comparisons about competitors.

- **DO NOT** tie the purchase of certain goods and services to the required purchase of additional goods or services without first contacting the legal department.

- **DO NOT** make exclusive dealing arrangements without first contacting the legal department.

1.1.1   Gun Jumping

As suggested above, there are certain general rules regarding information exchange among competitors, including competitors discussing possible joint activity. However, an especially sensitive opportunity for sharing information comes when the parties have agreed, at least in principal, to go forward with a merger or acquisition. It is important to remember that until the merger or acquisition has closed, the parties remain competitors, fully susceptible to all proscriptions of the antitrust laws, including the prohibition on sharing confidential information concerning price, cost, market strategies, and the like. This complicates matters as the parties do their due diligence, price the deal, and prepare for the best possible transition once the deal is final. When negotiations are far enough along that confidential, competitive information is required to be exchanged, there are certain safeguards (involvement of third parties, Chinese walls, and information compartmentalization) that can mitigate antitrust concerns. Premature sharing of competitively sensitive information[7] or prematurely taking over a component of the merger target's business can have serious consequences with millions of dollars in fines and penalties. Such premature information exchange is often called *gun jumping* and has received much attention by the DOJ and the FTC over the years.

Particularly suspicious are preclosing joint competitive activity, exchange of highly sensitive information, or interim agreements that give operational control or highly favorable terms to one party—because they are still competitors, all competitive business decisions still must be made independently. Gun jumping is not only subject to a claim under Section 1 of the Sherman Act, exposing the companies to treble damage claims,[8] but also to civil penalties under the premerger notification provisions of the Hart-Scott-Rodino (HSR) Act if the parties begin to implement the transaction prior to the termination of the Act's waiting periods.[9]

The DOJ and FTC have not promulgated official guidelines on improper gun jumping, although agency personnel have given speeches clarifying their views on the topic.[10] Deciding whether gun jumping has occurred is a fact-intensive inquiry examining a host of factors including: whether any competitive decisions were made unilaterally by the seller, imposed by the buyer, or some combination of the two; how the decisions affect the parties' competitiveness and any effect on competition in the market; and whether the decisions represent a material change in the business operations of the seller.

---

[7] For example, one hospital to a proposed merger faces rate negotiations with an insurance company that must be concluded prior to the actual closing date of the merger. Although it would be advantageous to know what that insurance company was paying the soon-to-be partner to the merger, sharing such rate information before the merger was complete would be a serious violation of antitrust law.

[8] *E.g.,* Omnicare, Inc. v. UnitedHealth Group, Inc., 629 F.3d 697 (7th Cir. 2011.) (In a private treble damage action alleging pre-merger conspiracy between merger participants to violate Section 1 of the Sherman Act, a motion to dismiss was denied although summary judgment was properly granted after extensive discovery and expert testimony.)

[9] 15 U.S.C. § 18a(g). For example, in 2009 Smithfield Foods, Inc., agreed to pay a $900,000 fine in connection with allegations that it prematurely asserted control of Premium Standard Farms, L.L.C.'s hog purchasing contracts before the merger of the two companies was consummated. United States v. Smithfield Foods, Inc., No. 1:10-CV-00120 (D.D.C. Jan. 21, 2009).

[10] *E.g.,* Blumenthal, W., "The Rhetoric of Gun-Jumping, Remarks before the Association of Corporate Council," Nov. 10, 2005 (*available at* http://www.ftc.gov/speeches/blumenthal/20051110gunjumping.pdf).

The general preclosing guidelines suggestions below highlight some concerns merging parties should keep in mind. Again, competitors cannot even appear to be coordinating any ongoing business activities until all antitrust approvals are received and the merger closes. Accordingly, even as parties are planning for the integration and efficient operation of the merged entity, they must operate as independent competitors.

In almost every case it is advisable that each party to the transaction identify a transition team, which will be insulated from operations personnel at either company. Members of the team should be from the strategic, not the operating, side of the business. Both parties generally, and the transition team in particular, should be familiar with the following working rules.

1.1.1.1   General Preclosing Guidelines

- Hands-off other companies' business operations.

    Neither party may limit the ability of the other to conduct its operations in the usual course of business. For example, in the case of an acquisition, the buyer must not involve itself in the seller's day-to-day business operations by imposing prices and terms of trade, strategies, purchasing decisions, capital outlay, product line or geographic expansion, research and development, advertising, or other business development.

- No coordinating business practices or strategies.

    The parties must not coordinate their production or distribution policies and practices, including processing, commercialization of goods, or the rendering of services.

- No discussion of, or joint communication to, customers.

    The parties must deal with their customers independently and may not hold themselves out to customers or suppliers as a combined entity until the actual closing of the deal. Each company must continue to separately develop market strategies, solicit business, and set prices and terms and conditions of trade. It is imperative that sales terms, prices, customers, and other marketing strategies must not be discussed by the parties prior to closing. As a general rule, counsel should be involved if joint meetings with customers are considered, including the parameters of such meetings.

- No co-mingling at internal meetings.

    It is important that the parties must not attend each other's internal meetings. They can generally observe day-to-day plant operations and review information during due dili-gence, but they may not share trade secrets and other pro-prietary information.

- Protection of a party's purchase.

    In the case of acquisition, the buyer can limit the seller from taking actions outside the ordinary course of business, such as major capital expenditures, in order to ensure that it obtains the agreed-upon assets. However, it is critical that the buyer not cross the line into managing the day-to-day operations of the seller.

- All business decisions to be made independently.

    The parties may make unilateral and independent decisions in anticipation of future joint operations and do what is nec-essary to carry out those decisions.

A couple of specific situations have attracted gun-jumping scrutiny in the past, so particular caution in these scenarios is advisable:

- Joint advertising efforts by two companies (e.g., radio stations) that might otherwise be permitted but, in the context of a deal, may be improper because they effectively combine the companies' market-ing operations prematurely.

- Day-to-day management of the to-be-acquired company by a vertically related buyer (e.g., management of a hospital by an acquir-ing hospital management service) while the acquisition is still pend-ing is a situation that must be dealt with carefully.

1.1.1.2   Guidelines Concerning Preclosing Information Exchanges

The parties will want data from each other to assist in planning for the integration of the businesses. Although information exchanges, like coordi-nated conduct, can lead to gun-jumping charges, deal partners can exchange a substantial amount of information without raising gun-jumping concerns.

Merging companies may share the following:

- Information in the public domain or of a type that is regularly or usu-ally disclosed to third parties, such as stock analysts;

- General information regarding operations, management, personnel, and human resources;

- Balance sheet and other financial data, including current and pro-jected sales, revenue, costs, and profits by broad product categories, and tax returns, as long as this information is necessary to prudent consideration of the transaction;

- Lists and descriptions of current products, manufacturing and distribution assets, distribution, and general business activities;
- Information regarding data processing, information and risk management, accounting, and computer systems;
- General information regarding existing joint ventures or similar relationships with third parties (giving due consideration to confidentiality obligations to third parties);
- Projected revenues and profits of merged operations for general, not specific, product lines;
- Aggregate customer information;
- Information regarding environmental risks; and
- Information regarding pending legal claims against the company.

Other competitively sensitive information should *only* be shared if there is a deal-related reason for doing so, and even then *only* with prior legal department approval. Of course, what constitutes "competitively sensitive" information will vary by industry, but, as a general rule, if management would be hesitant to disclose certain information with a competitor, that information should not be freely shared with a deal partner either. When competitively sensitive information is to be shared, both parties' legal departments should document and be able to justify all preclosing conduct and information exchanges with a deal-related purpose.

Without appropriate safeguards (such as third party collection of information, creation of Chinese walls, and information compartmentalization), merging companies *must not share* the following:

- Specific current or projected cost or profit information;
- Current or planned confidential business strategies, including marketing, pricing, production, bidding strategies, or strategic plans;
- Detailed sales figures by customer, customer lists, information about pending bids, or other customer-specific information including any particular other terms of sale and specific contracts (although historical customer information may be aggregated as long as the individual customers are not identifiable);
- Particular current and proposed customer and supplier contracts or conditions of trade, except that form contracts and contracts with pricing/deal terms redacted may be shared on a case-by-case basis depending on the deal-related reasons for disclosure; and
- Details about ongoing research and development efforts, especially about the development of new products (unless already public knowledge).

One legitimate purpose for the exchange of competitively sensitive information is joint preparation of a study examining postmerger efficiencies.

These studies are essential to the parties' due diligence and, in some instances, are the core of the companies' case for the merger and, if necessary, regulators. Nonetheless, it is apparent that efficiency studies could promote improper information exchanges; accordingly, the exchange of any competitively sensitive information, including its need, should be documented. Further, information should be accessible only to the due diligence or transition team or to outside consultants. In addition, whenever competitively sensitive information is going to be exchanged, companies are advised to enter into a nondisclosure agreement detailing the information to be exchanged and the identity of those who will have access to it.

Clearly, regulators are actively looking for gun-jumping violations. Although no bright line between proper and improper preclosing conduct has been drawn, the guidelines above should allow companies to begin lawfully planning integration efforts as soon as a deal is signed, so long as actual integration, including the unsupervised exchange of specific confidential competitive information, does not happen before the deal is formally and finally concluded.

1.2   IS APPROVAL NEEDED FROM THE FEDERAL OR STATE AGENCIES TO CONSUMMATE A MERGER?

Maybe. At the federal level, mergers of entities of a certain size and of a certain value must be reported to the Antitrust Division and FTC under the HSR Act.[11] As of 2011, under the HSR Act, a merger valued in excess of $66 million between one company with sales of at least $13.2 million and another company with assets or annual sales of more than $131.9 million is reportable to the FTC and DOJ and is subject to waiting requirements and agency investigation for approval. If the transaction is valued at greater than $263.8 million, it is reportable whatever the size of the entities involved. (The thresholds are subject to statutory annual adjustments.) Basically, any merger can be investigated by the agencies, but a merger meeting the threshold size levels must be reported to and cleared by the agencies to go forward.

In addition, in the healthcare area most states have statutes regulating merger activity. For example, over two-thirds of the states have a version of a Certificate of Need (CON) program meant to regulate and rationalize delivery of the state's healthcare, ensure that all communities are served, and ensure all facilities operate at peak efficiency. (Whether CONs tend to achieve this stated purpose is a matter of some debate.) Because a CON is by its nature governmental approval, it can be considered state action, immunizing the transaction from operation of the antitrust laws. Generally, CONs can be required for acquisitions, mergers, or expansions that, in the healthcare

---

[11]   15 U.S.C. § 18a (HSR Act).

market are possibly subject to threshold expenditure terms. Moreover, some states have laws requiring some form of state approval, usually from the state's Attorney General, if a not-for-profit hospital is merged or acquired.

1.3 WHAT IS A "VIRTUAL" MERGER? HOW DOES IT DIFFER FROM OTHER MERGERS?

Section 1 of the Sherman Act, 15 U.S.C. § 1, which prohibits certain agreements between competitors, can often pose significant problems depending on the nature of the arrangement between hospitals seeking to operate jointly. A fully consummated merger will avoid Section 1 issues because the resulting single entity is legally incapable of agreeing with itself to undertake any anticompetitive activity.[12]

However, where joint venture participants remain otherwise separate with independent economic interests and otherwise capable of independent decision making, their agreement to work together could be scrutinized under Section 1 for possible anticompetitive effects.[13] In such a case, and absent certain *per se* prohibitions (such as agreements between competitors on price), the agreement is scrutinized under the "rule of reason" to ascertain whether its procompetitive aspects, such as efficiencies and the ability to offer additional services neither hospital could offer on its own, outweigh any possible anticompetitive effects resulting from the hospitals working together.[14] For example, two separate, independent hospitals could not legally agree on the reimbursement rate for operating room time,[15] although their agreement to combine laundry facilities to achieve cost savings would probably pass antitrust muster.

1.3.1 Virtual Mergers

Virtual mergers (i.e., combinations in which the parties retain some managerial and financial independence while coordinating mutual operations) have, under certain circumstances, become an option for hospitals unable for political, practical, or religious reasons to consummate an actual merger. They or their parents typically retain ownership of assets and have significant

---

[12] *See, e.g.,* Copperweld Corp. v. Independence Tube Corp., 467 U.S. 752, 769 (1984); Healthamerica Pennsylvania, Inc. v. Susquehanna Health System, 278 F. Supp. 2d 423, 436 (M.D. Pa. 2003).

[13] *See, e.g.,* American Needle, Inc. v. National Football League, 560 U.S. 877, 885-887 (2010), 130 S.Ct. 2201, 2010 WL 2025207.

[14] *See, generally* Leegin Creative Leather Products, Inc. v. PSKS, Inc., 551 U.S. 877, 885-887, 127 S.Ct. 2705, 2712-2713 (2007) (explaining the "rule of reason" analysis).

[15] *E.g.,* Spitzer v. St. Francis Hospital, 94 F. Supp. 399, 414 (S.D.N.Y. 2000).

reserved powers. Some have been successful against antitrust challenge,[16] although some have not.[17] It is probable that virtual mergers would be viewed in the same manner as "real" mergers by the Antitrust Division of the DOJ and the FTC, the primary governmental agencies charged with antitrust law enforcement.[18] Critical to a virtual merger's legality, at least from a Section 1 standpoint, is that the hospitals "align their economic interest" as closely as possible so that they can together be considered a single actor acting wholly unilaterally and, therefore, not subject to Section 1.

1.3.1.1 Susquehanna Health System

In *Healthamerica Pennsylvania, Inc. v. Susquehanna Health System,* two competing hospital systems created an alliance whereby they maintained their separate identities, responsibility for their missions and values, governance, credentials, medical staff issues, and quality assurance of their respective hospitals. However, virtually all other aspects of their operations were merged, including pricing and managed care negotiation. The arrangement survived antitrust attack by a managed healthcare plan and various healthcare insurers.

The alliance had been officially established pursuant to a consent order entered into between the hospitals on the one hand and the Pennsylvania Attorney General on the other. Apparently, the parties had negotiated the terms of the consent order prior to any litigation.

The court ruled that, as constituted, the alliance was essentially one economic entity incapable of agreeing with itself under Section 1 of the Sherman Act and granted summary judgment for the defendants. Although the court did not discuss the fact that the alliance had been sanctioned by the state Attorney General, and that pursuant to reporting requirements there was to be a certain amount of state supervision, the involvement of the Attorney General may have been an important aspect of the agreement creating the alliance.

---

[16] *E.g.,* Healthamerica Pennsylvania, Inc. v. Susquehanna Health System, 278 F. Supp. 2d 423 (M.D. Pa. 2003) (discussed below).

[17] *E.g.,* St. Francis Hospital, 94 F. Supp. 2d at 422. In St. Francis, two hospitals entered into a small number of discrete joint ventures with the New York Attorney General's approval. In operating the joint ventures, the hospitals ended up combining other functions, such as negotiating with payors and otherwise operating more closely than originally envisioned. The Attorney General sued and won a summary judgment that the hospitals had violated Section 1.

[18] *See, e.g.,* "Virtual Mergers of Hospitals: When Does the *Per Se* Rule Apply?," Mark J. Botti, Assistant Chief, Antitrust Division, presentation before the American Health Lawyers Association (Feb. 14, 2000); Jeff Miles, *The Importance of Integration in Healthcare Antitrust Counseling?,* AHLA Health Lawyers News, Mar. 2004.

It may be possible to structure a virtual merger that does not include all of the elements involved in the Susquehanna alliance, but clearly the more integration that occurs and the more the involved hospitals act as one economic entity, the less vulnerable joint operation would be to antitrust challenge.

From an antitrust standpoint, complete financial integration, including the sharing of profits and losses and operational integration of assets, finances, and possibly consolidation of debt, is optimal as it evidences that the entity is acting as one economic unit. In addition, even if they retain separate liability for their past debts, the hospitals should consider making significant annual capital contributions to the alliance to promote mutual interests. Hospitals also should consider cross-guarantees of loans and future bond issues. By such means, the hospitals would demonstrate sufficient financial interdependence that they have formed a single entity and, therefore, should be subject to more favorable antitrust treatment.[19]

Where feasible, administration, back-office operations, specialty services, and operational expenses (e.g., laundry and linen) should be consolidated. To prevent the individual interest of one hospital from barring such consolidation after closing, the parties should consider delegating the authority over such consolidation to a single board composed of individuals from both institutions. In addition, activities such as contracting with suppliers and union negotiations should be consolidated, with oversight delegated to the board.

Such delegation to a single board has two consequences for the transaction's antitrust assessment. First, the antitrust agencies will be more likely to recognize the transaction as a merger if the board can implement companywide cost-cutting measures. Second, concrete commitments to eliminate duplicative operations will confirm that the transaction's goal is to achieve efficiencies rather than anticompetitive advantages.

Additionally, to demonstrate a commitment to efficient operations, and thus demonstrate good faith from an antitrust perspective, the hospitals should consider extending reciprocal privileges to medical staffs. Moreover, if feasible, actually combining medical staffs would underscore the commitment to truly join interests. To deal with the cooperation impediments among the medical staffs, the hospitals should work closely with their physicians to gradually mesh the staffs. To facilitate this process, the hospitals may form a physician committee with representation from both hospitals. In sum, if the

---

[19] Consistent with the "single entity" goal, the parties should be careful of reservation of important powers—such as control of capital spending issues or veto power over major business decisions—and super majority board requirements. Obviously, any provisions in the arrangement that allow one of the participants to block alliance initiatives in furtherance of individual interest detract from the goal of economic and business unity.

hospitals do not completely integrate in the sense of a full merger, consolidation, or change of control, they should operate as much as possible as a single corporation.

Whether an actual merger would survive antitrust scrutiny is largely a question of how powerful the merged entity would become—for example, merger of the only two acute care hospitals in a given geographic area is not likely to withstand antitrust challenge. Whether a virtual merger would survive antitrust scrutiny asks the additional question of whether the parties' economic interests are sufficiently fused that they function as one economic entity.

1.4 HOW DO THE FEDERAL ANTITRUST AGENCIES ANALYZE WHETHER TO CHALLENGE MERGERS? DOES THE ANALYSIS DIFFER DEPENDING ON WHETHER THE MERGER IS BETWEEN HOSPITALS, PHYSICIANS, HOSPITALS AND PHYSICIANS, OR HEALTH PLANS?

In determining whether to challenge a merger in any industry under Section 7 of the Clayton Act,[20] the FTC and Antitrust Division apply their *Horizontal Merger Guidelines* (*Merger Guidelines*) (completely revised and updated in August 2010)[21] as well as relevant merger case law. The *Merger Guidelines* are not binding precedent on the courts but are highly persuasive, and courts apply them frequently in deciding merger cases.[22] The framework for analyzing mergers does not vary depending on the industry in which the merger occurs, although the analysis must always consider and account for the industry's particular characteristics and the likely competitive issues that mergers in different industries can raise.

As the *Merger Guidelines* state, the ultimate question the agencies attempt to answer in every merger investigation is whether the merger is likely to "create, enhance, or entrench market power or to facilitate its exercise."[23] Those effects most frequently result from *horizontal mergers*—that is, mergers between competitors, such as two hospitals providing overlapping services in overlapping geographic areas—because horizontal mergers directly reduce

---

[20] 15 U.S.C. § 18.

[21] U.S. Dep't of Justice & Federal Trade Comm'n, *Horizontal Merger Guidelines* (Aug. 19, 2010) (*Merger Guidelines*), *available at* http://www.ftc.gov/os/2010/08/100819hmg.pdf.

[22] Chicago Iron & Bridge Co. v. FTC, 534 F.3d 410, 434 (5th Cir. 2008).

[23] *Merger Guidelines* § 1.

the number of competitors in a market. This may permit the merging firms (and perhaps other competitors in the market) to raise their prices or reduce their quality in ways that harm consumers.

Less frequently, *vertical mergers*—that is, those between suppliers and customers or parties in a similar upstream/downstream relationship—can also raise antitrust issues. A hospital's acquisition of physician practices, for example, is a vertical merger because physicians are suppliers of patients to hospitals. Here, the most frequent concern is *foreclosure* of other competitors from the market. For example, if the acquired physician practice accounts for a large percentage of all hospital admissions in an area and, after the acquisition, that practice admits its patients only to the acquiring hospital, competing hospitals may be foreclosed from such a significant percentage of revenue that they become weakened or nonexistent competitors, unable to constrain the market power of the acquiring hospital. Moreover, a merger can have both horizontal and vertical aspects. For example, if the hospital acquiring a physician practice already employs physicians in the acquired practice's specialty, the merger is both horizontal and vertical and must be analyzed as such.[24]

Horizontal mergers can have seller-side effects, buyer-side effects, or both. Hospital mergers typically raise seller-side issues that the merger may provide the merged hospital with market power enabling it, in selling hospital services, to raise prices to health plans. However, the merger can raise buyer-side issues as well; for example where, the merging hospitals employ a large percentage of nurses in the area the merger may provide the merged hospital with *monopsony* power, i.e., buyer side monopoly power, as a purchaser of nurses' services and, thus, the ability to lower wages anticompetitively. Health plan mergers can also raise both seller-side issues (the ability to raise premiums in selling health insurance) and buyer-side issues (in purchasing the services of physicians and hospitals).[25]

The *Merger Guidelines* explain that mergers can generate three general types of competitive concern; it is important to determine which of those concerns warrants the greatest attention. First, the merger may provide the merged firm with sufficient market power, by itself, to raise prices anticompetitively—a problem the *Merger Guidelines* refer to as "unilateral effects."[26] Second, the merger may result in a market that is so highly concentrated[27]

---

[24] For an example, *see* HTI Health Servs., Inc. v. Quorum Health Group, Inc., 960 F. Supp. 1104 (S.D. Miss. 1997).

[25] For an example, *see* United States v. UnitedHealth Group, Inc., 2006-1 Trade Cas. (CCH) ¶ 75,255 (D.D.C. 2006) (consent decree and competitive impact statement).

[26] *Merger Guidelines* § 6.

[27] The level of market concentration is a function of the number of firms in the relevant market and their sizes relative to one another—the fewer the number of firms and the

that the firms in the market engage in interdependent competitive decision making. For example, no one may lower prices to compete because they recognize that if they do so, their competitors will do the same and they will gain no market share. Or they may raise prices, believing or knowing that their competitors will do the same, so their price increase will result in little lost business. The *Merger Guidelines* refer to this concern as "coordinated effects" through "coordinated interaction."[28] Finally, in rare situations, the merger may result in a single firm with sufficient market power to engage in predatory or exclusionary conduct toward other competitors, thus increasing the merged firm's market power even further.[29]

The agencies' 2010 *Merger Guidelines* substantially rewrote, revamped, and updated the agencies' 1992 merger guidelines.[30] In assessing or predicting the competitive effects of mergers, the older guidelines (and the courts) generally implemented an eight-step, progressive, linear, analytical framework, with steps taken in the following order:

1. ***Define the relevant product and geographic markets.*** The methodologies for defining relevant markets are beyond the scope of this chapter.[31] But in analyzing hospital mergers, most courts have defined the *relevant product market* as the sale of inpatient acute-care hospital services, excluding outpatient services and the services of specialty and Veterans Administration hospitals. The definition of the product market, however, depends particularly on the overlapping services of the merging hospitals and, depending on the facts, may be limited to individual hospital services, such as obstetrics.[32] Under the agencies'—and more frequently now the courts'—so-called *hypothetical monopolist* methodology, the product market includes only those services over which a hypothetical monopolist could profitably raise

---

greater their disparity in size, the higher the level of market concentration. Economic theory and some empirical work posit that, all else equal, the higher the level of market concentration, the more likely that prices will rise above the competitive level. *See generally* FTC v. H.J. Heinz Co., 246 F.3d 708, 724 n.23 (D.C. Cir. 2001).

[28] *Merger Guidelines* § 7.

[29] *Id.* § 2 & Ex. 2.

[30] For an excellent and helpful discussion of the 2010 *Merger Guidelines*, including their differences from the 1992 merger guidelines, *see* Carl Shapiro, *The 2010 Horizontal Merger Guidelines: From Hedgehog to Fox in Forty Years*, 77 Antitrust L. J. 49 (2010).

[31] *See* Chapter III, "Relevant Markets for Health Care," in American Bar Association, Section of Antitrust Law, *Antitrust Health Care Handbook* (4th ed. 2010).

[32] *See, e.g.*, FTC v. ProMedica Health Sys., Inc., 2011 WL 1219281 (N.D. Ohio Mar. 29, 2011) (carving out a separate relevant product market for obstetric services in a hospital merger case).

prices because too few customers would turn to alternative sources to defeat the price increase.[33] The relevant market need not include *all* substitutes for the merging firms' products as some merger decisions hold.[34] Under that same methodology, the relevant geographic market includes only that area over which a hypothetical monopolist of the relevant product could profitably increase the price because too few customers would turn to more distant sources to defeat a hypothetical price increase—not the larger area that includes every firm that competes with the merging parties.[35]

2. ***Based on the definition of the relevant market, identify market participants.*** Under the *Merger Guidelines*, market participants include not only competitors in the relevant market but also firms that earn revenues from sales in the relevant market.[36]

3. ***Calculate the market shares of market participants.***

4. ***Calculate the merged firm's postmerger market share.*** This figure can be important if the potential concern from the merger is unilateral effects but less important if the concern is coordinated effects.

5. ***Calculate the level of postmerger market concentration and the degree to which the merger would increase that level.*** These figures are particularly important if the potential concern from the merger is coordinated effect but less important if the concern is unilateral effects.

   The *Merger Guidelines* and the courts employ the Herfindahl-Hirschman Index (HHI) to measure market concentration. To calculate the postmerger HHI, (i) calculate the market shares of the merging firms, (ii) square the market share of each market participant, and (iii) sum the squares. This can result in a maximum HHI value of 10,000 (i.e., 100^2) when the merging firms are the only two market participants. To calculate the degree to which the merger increases the HHI, multiply the market shares of the merging firms by each other, and multiply that product by 2. So if firms with 10 percent and 5 percent shares merge, the HHI will increase by 100.

6. ***Determine whether the merger is prima facie, or rebuttably presumed, unlawful based on court decisions and the* Merger Guidelines.** Court decisions provide that if the postmerger market share or postmerger level of concentration resulting from the merger

---

[33] *Merger Guidelines* § 4.1.1.
[34] *Id.*
[35] *Id.* § 4.2.
[36] *Id.* § 5.1.

is sufficiently high, a rebuttable presumption arises that the merger is unlawful.[37] The *Merger Guidelines* provide benchmarks against which the market concentration level resulting from the merger can be compared to preliminarily assess the degree of antitrust risk.

According to the *Guidelines*, a market is *unconcentrated* if the postmerger HHI is below 1,500 (about seven equal-size firms). Mergers that result in unconcentrated markets "ordinarily require no further analysis."[38] In effect, this is an antitrust safety zone. Markets with HHIs between 1,500 and 2,500 are "moderately concentrated," normally requiring further analysis only if the merger increases the HHI by 100 or more. A market with an HHI of 2,500 or more is "highly concentrated." A merger resulting in this high concentration level typically requires further investigation if the increase in the HHI is between 100 and 200, but the *Merger Guidelines* provide that the merger "will be presumed to be likely to enhance market power," and thus rebuttably presumed unlawful, if it increases the HHI by more than 200 points.[39]

7. *Determine whether the concern, if any, arises from potential coordinated interaction or unilateral effects (or both), and analyze the likely effects as explained by the courts and in the* **Merger Guidelines**.

Coordinated effects. If the potential concern is coordinated effects, the agencies examine factors related to the (i) ease of coordinated decision making among competitors, (ii) profitability of successful coordination, and (iii) difficulty of competitors cheating on the coordination without detection. As to the third factor, if competitors can secretly cheat by, for example, lowering price without detection by their competitors, coordination among them becomes unstable and unsuccessful. The single most important variable in predicting the likelihood of coordinated effects is the market concentration level. But the agencies also examine a number of other variables (listed in the *Merger Guidelines*) shedding light on the three factors.[40]

Unilateral effects. If the potential concern is unilateral effects, the analysis depends on whether the products of the merging parties are differentiated (for example, hospital and physician services) or

---

[37] *E.g.*, Polypore Int'l, Inc., 2010 WL 5132519 at *13 (FTC Dec. 13, 2010).

[38] *Merger Guidelines* § 5.3.

[39] *Id.*

[40] *Id.* §§ 7.1, 7.2.

undifferentiated.[41] In the case of differentiated products, concern is most acute when the services of merging parties—for example, two merging hospitals—are the first and second choices of a large number of customers (health plans and patients) such that if the merged firm raised prices at one hospital, a large percentage of its customers would choose the other rather than other area hospitals—in antitrust jargon, if the diversion ratio from one of the merging parties to the other is high. In this situation, lost revenues from diverting patients are internalized within the merged hospital rather than lost to competitors; depending on the contribution margins, the price increase may be profitable.[42] Recent hospital-merger challenges have focused on unilateral effects/differentiated products concerns.[43]

The *Merger Guidelines* provide two de facto safety zones, whether the potential concern from the merger is unilateral effects, coordinated interaction, or both: (i) where the postmerger HHI is 1,500 or less, and (ii) regardless of the postmerger HHI, where the increase in the HHI from the merger is less than 100. In addition, Statement 1 of the agencies' *Statements of Antitrust Enforcement Policy in Health Care*[44] provides an explicit antitrust safety zone for very small hospital mergers (generally, one of the hospitals has less than 100 beds and an average daily census of less than 40 patients).

8. *If the merger is prima facie unlawful, examine qualitative factors that may rebut the presumption.* These can be broken down into (1) barriers to entry by new firms and expansion by incumbent firms,

---

[41] *Merger Guidelines* §§ 6.1, 6.3. *Differentiated products* are products that are sufficiently interchangeable so they are part of the same relevant product market but sufficiently different that customers have relatively strong preferences for one over the other. The services of different hospitals, for example, are differentiated based on a number of variables, including location, array of services, quality of services, quality of medical staffs, amenities, religious affiliation, and the like.

[42] For a helpful explanation of unilateral-effect/differentiated products merger theory, *see* Carl Shapiro, *Mergers with Differentiated Products*, Antitrust, Spring 1996, at 23. For an example of its application in hospital merger analysis, *see* Evanston Nw. Healthcare Corp., 2007-2 Trade Cas. (CCH) ¶ 75,814 at 108,585-86 (FTC Aug. 2, 2007).

[43] In addition to the *Evanston Northwestern Healthcare* decision, *see* the FTC's administrative complaint in Inova Health System Foundation, *available at* http://www.ftc.gov/os/adjpro/d9326/080509admincomplaint.pdf.

[44] *Available at* http://www.ftc.gov/bc/healthcare/industryguide/policy/statement1.htm.

(2) efficiencies from the merger, and (3) the likely future competitive strength of one or both of the merging parties:[45]

Entry and expansion. If new firms would enter the market immediately or incumbent firms could expand output in light of an attempt by the merged firm to raise prices, even a merger to monopoly would raise no antitrust problem—if the amount of new output would offset the merged firm's reduction in output necessary for it to raise its prices.[46] But the *Merger Guidelines* require that entry be "timely," "likely," and "sufficient" to offset the potential anticompetitive merger effects.[47] To be timely, entry must be sufficiently rapid that any price increase by the merged firm would be unprofitable. The agencies' 1992 guidelines provided that entry is timely if it occurred within two years; unfortunately, the 2010 *Merger Guidelines* provide no similar objective benchmark. To be likely, entry must be profitable, taking into account that entry would likely lower the price that new entrants could obtain; and to be sufficient, entry must counteract the competitive concerns from the merger. In the case of unilateral-effects analysis, the ability of competitors to reposition their products or services to compete more directly with those of the merged is analogous to new entry or expansion.

In the case of hospital mergers, especially in states with CON laws, sufficient new entry or expansion is unlikely. Even absent CON regulation, the time necessary to plan and build a new hospital and for it to become a viable competitor is likely to be lengthy. Barriers also exist into both health plan and physician markets. Barriers into the former include the need to develop the necessary provider networks and the necessity to gain substantial numbers of members to obtain significant discounts from providers.[48] And while it may be easy for physicians to move into a new area, establishing a viable practice, especially for specialists, can take quite a while.

---

[45] One rebuttal factor that the courts have almost universally rejected in the context of mergers between nonprofit hospitals is the argument that the parties have no incentive to exercise market power because of their nonprofit status. *See, e.g.,* FTC v. University Health, Inc., 938 F.2d 1206, 1224 (11th Cir. 1991).

[46] *See Merger Guidelines* § 9.

[47] *Id.*

[48] *See generally* Christine Varney, Assistant Attorney General, Antitrust Division, "Antitrust and Health Care," prepared remarks before the ABA/AHLA Antitrust in Healthcare Conference (May 10, 2010), *available at* http:/www.justice.gov/atr/public/speeches/258898.pdf.

Efficiencies from the merger. Increased efficiency is the goal of most mergers, and these can offset the merger's potential anticompetitive effects. The agencies, as a practical matter, define *efficiencies* broadly to include not only integration resulting in lower costs, but also improvements in quality, new services, and greater access—in effect, anything that benefits consumers.

But the *Merger Guidelines'* requirements for the efficiencies to count in favor of the merger are strict. In general, the efficiencies must (1) be merger specific—that is, they would not be achieved absent the merger; (2) be verified; and (3) not result from "anticompetitive reductions in output or service."[49] As to verification, the merging parties bear the burden to show the agency

1. the likelihood that they will actually achieve the efficiencies,
2. the magnitude of the efficiencies,
3. when each efficiency will be achieved,
4. the cost of achieving each efficiency, and
5. how each efficiency will enhance competition.

Ultimately, according to the *Merger Guidelines* and court decisions,[50] the efficiencies must be sufficient to offset any price increase resulting from the transaction, suggesting, as some decisions have held,[51] that the benefits of the efficiencies must be passed on to consumers in the form of, for example, lower prices.

Efficiency reports and arguments typically play a major role in attempting to convince an agency not to challenge a hospital merger that otherwise raises antitrust concern. Efficiencies clearly count in favor of the merger, but as one court noted in a recent hospital merger decision, "No court . . . has found efficiencies sufficient to rescue an otherwise illegal merger."[52] And the *Merger Guidelines* themselves note that efficiencies rarely, if ever, justify a merger to monopoly or duopoly.

The merging firms' future competitive strength. Merger analysis focuses on the merger's effect on future competition, and sometimes a firm's current market share or competitive strength fails to reflect its future share or strength.[53] As a result, the agencies examine whether one or both of the firms are, as a technical matter, a "failing firm"; or, even if not, whether the financial

---

[49] *Merger Guidelines* § 10.

[50] *E.g.*, FTC v. CCC Holdings, Inc., 605 F. Supp. 2d 26, 74 (D.D.C. 2009).

[51] *E.g.*, FTC v. University Health, Inc., 938 F.2d 1206, 1222 (11th Cir. 1991).

[52] FTC v. ProMedica Health Sys., Inc., 2011-1 Trade Cas. (CCH) ¶ 77,395 at *57 (N.D. Ohio Mar. 29, 2011).

[53] *E.g.*, United States v. Gen. Dynamics Corp., 415 U.S. 486 (1974).

position of one or both, in the near future, will decline to the extent that its current market share significantly overstates its future ability to compete and, thus, overstates the merger's likely effect on competition.

That one of the firms is a failing firm is a dispositive affirmative defense to a merger challenge. But the requirements for proving the defense are strict. The merging parties must prove that (i) the failing party will not be able to meet its financial obligations in the future—i.e., that it is insolvent; (ii) it cannot reorganize successfully under Chapter 11 of the Bankruptcy Act; and (ii) it unsuccessfully sought a merger partner whose acquisition of it would have less of an adverse effect on competition than the partner it chose.[54] Rarely can the parties sustain the failing firm defense, but it was successful in one hospital merger case.[55]

Parties to problematic hospital mergers frequently argue that although neither hospital is failing in the sense above, one is a flailing hospital or weakened competitor in the sense that its competitive strength has declined and will continue to decline absent the merger. If true, this fact is not a dispositive defense but only one factor that the agencies and courts consider in rebuttal to a prima facie case. Several courts have stated, however, that it is perhaps the weakest rebuttal factor of all.[56] How weak must the flailing hospital be for the argument to carry the day? The answer is not clear; but in one recent hospital-merger decision, the court explained that the evidence would have to predict that the flailing firm's share would decrease to a level negating the government's prima facie case.[57]

Although the courts, at present, usually follow the analysis pathway described above, the 2010 *Merger Guidelines* explain that the agencies, in assessing mergers, may not. Rather, they will consider any and all evidence in any order that sheds light on the merger's likely (or actual, if the merger has been consummated) effect on competition.[58] The agencies need not begin with market definition; indeed, in some situations—for example, where the merger has been consummated for some time and there is evidence of its actual effect on prices—it may not be necessary to even define a relevant market[59] because the only

---

[54]   *Merger Guidelines* § 11.

[55]   Cal. v. Sutter Health Sys., 130 F. Supp. 2d 1109, 1133-37(N.D. Cal. 2001).

[56]   *E.g.*, Kaiser Aluminum & Chem. Co. v. FTC, 652 F.2d 1324, 1339 (7th Cir. 1981).

[57]   FTC v. ProMedica Health Sys., Inc., 2011 WL 1219281 at *58 (N.D. Ohio, Mar. 29, 2011).

[58]   *Merger Guidelines* § 2 (explaining that the "Agencies consider any reasonably available and reliable evidence to address the central question of whether a merger may substantially lessen competition").

[59]   *See* Evanston Nw. Healthcare Corp., 2007-2 Trade Cas. (CCH) ¶ 75,814 at 108,586; 108,608 (FTC Aug. 2, 2007).

purpose to do so is to help predict the merger's effect on competition. An actual postmerger price increase resulting from the merger proves the requisite adverse effect on competition; under the hypothetical monopolist framework for defining relevant markets, it also shows that the merging firm's products, by themselves, constitute the relevant product market.[60] The *Merger Guidelines* note, however, that the agencies normally will define one or more relevant markets,[61] perhaps because that requirement is so entrenched in the merger case law.[62]

In general, relying on the 2010 *Merger Guidelines*, the agencies apply a more holistic approach than under the previous guidelines, often creating econometric models to predict the merger's direct effect on competition, relying on natural experiments (for example, actual effects under similar circumstances elsewhere), considering the actual effects of consummated mergers where there are sufficient data, and considering the views of the merging parties' customers and competitors about the merger's probable effect. As a result, although market concentration and share statistics continue to play an important role in merger analysis, they play a lesser role than in the past or under the agencies' previous merger guidelines. This reliance on so many varied factors may result in a more robust analysis, but it makes counseling clients significantly more difficult than where concentration and market-share statistics played the dominant role in the agencies' decision whether to challenge the transaction.

1.5 WHAT ARE THE CIRCUMSTANCES UNDER WHICH THE GOVERNMENT CAN CHALLENGE, RETROSPECTIVELY, A HOSPITAL MERGER?

The answer to this question is easy: the government can challenge a merger any time for any reason. As the hospitals involved in *Evanston Northwestern Healthcare Corporation*[63] learned, even prior approval by an agency will not insulate the results of a hospital merger from possible future action by the FTC or DOJ (or, indeed, a state agency.)[64]

---

[60] *Merger Guidelines* § 4.

[61] *Id.*

[62] *E.g.*, FTC v. Lundbeck, _____ F.3d _____, 2011 WL 3629347 at *2 (8th Cir. Aug. 19, 2011). This is so even when the agencies create and apply econometric models that predict the price effect of a merger without the need to define a relevant market. *See* City of New York v. Group Health, Inc., _____ F.3d _____, 2011 WL 3625097 at *6 (2d Cir. Aug. 18, 2011).

[63] *See* Evanston Nw. Healthcare Corp., 2007-2 Trade Cas. (CCH) ¶ 75,814 (FTC Aug. 2, 2007).

[64] The *time of suit* doctrine holds that the legality of a merger or acquisition should be determined at the time of suit rather than at the time the transaction was consummated.

Indeed, *Evanston* is a cautionary tale. The FTC, having conducted a pre-merger investigation pursuant to the HSR Act, decided not to challenge Evanston Northwestern Healthcare Corp.'s (ENH) acquisition of Highland Park Hospital. Four years later, however, the agency filed an administrative complaint against ENH, alleging that the merger was anticompetitive in violation of Section 7 of the Clayton Act, having resulted in dramatic reimbursement rate increases by managed care companies. The FTC ultimately agreed not to order divestiture, insisting instead on complete separation of managed care negotiations by the pre-merger entities. The Commission warned, however, that not requiring divestiture was unusual and that it would not hesitate in the future to order hospitals that merged in violation of Section 7 to "unscramble the eggs."

More recently, in January 2011, the FTC filed an administrative complaint against ProMedica Health System, Inc., challenging Toledo, Ohio-based ProMedica's acquisition of St. Luke's Hospital in Maumee, Ohio.[65] The FTC claims that after the acquisition, ProMedica controls "nearly 60% of the general acute-care inpatient hospital services in Lucas County and over 80% of the market for obstetrical services, as measured by patient days."[66] Importantly, the Complaint cites to "internal strategic plans" that show that a "principal motivation for the Acquisition was to gain enhanced bargaining leverage with health plans and the ability to raise prices for services."[67] The Complaint seeks complete divestiture, which may be less harmful to the institutions because complete integration of St. Luke's into the ProMedica Health System was delayed pursuant to an earlier FTC "hold separate" order.

Basically, significant postmerger rate increases or other indicia of anticompetitive activity will excite agency interest, and the fact that a particular acquisition or merger survived agency review at one time is no indication that it would do so again. Consummated mergers are always subject to later challenge, even if previously cleared under the HSR process.

Thus, for example, the Government was successful in challenging E.I duPont de Nemours & Co.'s purchase of stock in General Motors made some 30 years before suit was filed. United States v. E.I. duPont de Nemours & Co., 353 U.S. 586 (1957).

[65] In the Matter of ProMedica Health System, Inc., FTC Dist. No. 9346, *filed*, January 6, 2011. The district court granted the FTC's request for a preliminary injunction against the consummation of the merger pending completion of the FTC's administrative and legal challenge to the acquisition. *See*, FTC v. ProMedica Health Sys., Inc., 2011 WL 1219281 (N.D. Mar. 29, 2011).

[66] *Id.* at ¶ 5.

[67] *Id.* at ¶ 2.

2
Medical Staff and Peer Review

Mark L. Mattioli, Esquire
Marshall Dennehey Warner Coleman Goggin PC

Many healthcare antitrust suits arise as a result of medical staff relations issues. Although the routine cases where a physician's privileges were terminated due to competency-based issues or disruptive behavior are largely unsuccessful, a more recent trend is to allege that the physician was excluded from the hospital because he or she was viewed as a competitive threat to the hospital and/or some of its physicians. The physician will allege that the discipline was the result of a sham peer review process instigated by the physician's competitors who desired to exclude the physician from the hospital. Although the number of successful cases is still rare, the courts seem more willing to entertain these types of cases because they involve more traditional notions of antitrust law.

This chapter explores some of common antitrust issues that are encountered in staff privilege disputes. Given the increased competition between physicians and institutional providers, such issues will continue to arise.

2.1   CAN A HOSPITAL "CONSPIRE" WITH ITS MEDICAL STAFF WITH REGARD TO A PEER REVIEW PROCEEDING?

A crucial issue in peer review proceedings is the economic relationship between and among the hospital and its medical staff and physician members: Are they a single economic entity and, therefore, incapable of conspiring in violation of Section 1 of the Sherman Act, or are they separate economic entities whose joint activities may constitute a conspiracy in restraint of trade?. As will be discussed, Section 1 claims require that there be two independent actors who are capable of conspiring. The question then becomes whether a physician who is serving on a peer review committee can conspire with the hospital.

The majority rule is that a hospital cannot conspire with its medical staff where the medical staff is conducting a legitimate quality review to assess the competency or conduct of a physician on staff at the hospital. This position is based on the doctrine of intra-corporate immunity as articulated by the United States Supreme Court in *Copperweld Co. v. Independence Tube Corp.*[1] There, the Court held that a parent corporation could not conspire, for antitrust purposes, with its wholly-owned subsidiary as the entities were not separate economic competitors. Rather, they acted for a unified economic goal seeking to enhance the organization's goals as a whole.

The leading case discussing intra-corporate immunity in the medical staff context is *Oksanen v. Page Mem'l Hosp.*[2] There, the Fourth Circuit, following a number of other Circuits, held that a hospital was unable to conspire with its medical staff regarding peer review functions because the medical staff was acting as an agent of the hospital for purposes of reviewing the physician's credentials. Stated the court:

> In effect, the medical staff was working as the [Hospital] Board's agent under an "internal 'agreement' to implement a single, unitary firm's policies" of evaluating the conduct and competence of those to whom the hospital extended privileges.[3]

An important consideration in determining whether a hospital and its medical staff are capable of conspiring is whether the hospital authorized the physicians to act for the hospital in conducting a review of the physician. Where, for example, the physicians are acting unilaterally and outside of the normal peer review channels, their actions may not be covered under the cloak of intra-corporate immunity. In *Oltz v. St. Peter's Community Hosp.*,[4] one of the few cases to impose antitrust liability, the Ninth Circuit Court of Appeals held that a hospital was able to conspire with members of its medical staff where the medical staff acted independently in attempting to coerce a hospital to abandon its contract with a nurse anesthetist and instead enter into an exclusive contract with them.[5]

Even if intra-corporate immunity appears established, an exception may apply: The *independent personal stake exception* applies when an agent, who would otherwise be expected to be aligned with the corporation's economic interests, instead acts for his own personal benefit. A typical example is an

---

[1]   467 U.S. 752 (1984).

[2]   945 F.2d 696 (4th Cir. 1991), *cert. denied,* 502 U.S. 1074 (1992). *Compare* Bolt v. Halifax Hosp. Medical Center, 851 F.2d 1273, 1280 (11th Cir. 1988) (hospital and individual members of the medical staff are separate actors who can conspire for purposes of Section 1).

[3]   *Id.* at 703.

[4]   861 F.2d 1440 (9th Cir. 1988).

[5]   Although not discussed, a relevant factor also may have been that there were no real quality-of-care issues with the nurse anesthetist raised in *Oltz.*

agent with a financial interest that will benefit from the corporation's proposed action. In the medical staff context, plaintiffs sometimes use the independent personal stake exception to establish conspiracy by arguing that rival physicians used the peer review process to exclude a competitor to further the rivals' own practices and not for competency or behavioral reasons.

The success of the independent personal stake exception to establish a conspiracy may depend on who makes the ultimate decisions concerning the plaintiff's privileges. The court in *Oksanen*, for example, rejected the personal stake exception argument because it was the hospital—not the rival physicians—that made the ultimate decisions concerning the plaintiff's privileges. As explained by the court:

> Here, by contrast, the medical staff had no such control. "To give advice when asked by the decision maker is not equivalent to being the decision maker itself." The Board of Trustees at Page Memorial requested and encouraged the medical staff to take corrective action against Oksanen. The Board in the end retained authority over staff privilege decisions at Page Memorial. Because the challenged decision was subject to review by the hospital and because decision-making authority in Dr. Oksanen's case was dispersed among a number of individuals, the personal stake exception is inapplicable.[6]

Thus, the majority view is that a hospital cannot conspire with medical staff members who are conducting peer review in an official capacity on that hospital's behalf. Actions outside of the peer review process, including efforts to control corporate decisions for personal gain, may not be immune from conspiracy allegations. To protect peer review participants, it is important that their authority be delineated so as to avoid an argument that the participants were acting independently and, therefore, outside of the peer review context, and that any financial conflicts be disclosed to the hospital board.

2.2   WHAT IMMUNITIES ARE AVAILABLE TO PEER REVIEW COMMITTEE MEMBERS TO PROTECT THEM FROM ANTITRUST LIABILITY? HOW CAN MEMBERS TAKE ADVANTAGE OF THOSE IMMUNITIES?

The primary protection that is available to hospitals and participants in the medical staff credentialing process is the Health Care Quality Improvement Act (HCQIA) of 1986.[7] HCQIA provides limited immunity from damages

---

[6]   945 F.2d at 70506.

[7]   42 U.S.C. § 11001 *et seq.*

provided certain procedural requirements are met, namely that the provider is given minimum due process rights. HCQIA presumes that these requirements have been met and puts the burden on the disciplined physician to establish that the conditions for immunity have not been met.

2.2.1   What Does HCQIA Require?

To be entitled to immunity under HCQIA, a "professional" review action must be taken:[8]

(1) in the reasonable belief that the action was in the furtherance of quality healthcare,

(2) after a reasonable effort to obtain the facts of the matter,

(3) after adequate notice and hearing procedures are afforded to the physician involved or after such other procedures as are fair to the physician under the circumstances, and

(4) in the reasonable belief that the action was warranted by the facts known after such reasonable effort to obtain facts and after meeting the requirement of paragraph (3). A professional review action shall be presumed to have met the preceding standards necessary for the protection set out in section 411(a) [42 USCS § 11111(a)] unless the presumption is rebutted by a preponderance of the evidence.

The level of due process required for the presumption to apply is far less than is required in a court of law. Rather, the procedures are set out as follows[9]:

(1) Notice of proposed action. The physician has been given notice stating—

(A) (i)   that a professional review action has been proposed to be taken against the physician,

(ii) reasons for the proposed action,

(B) (i)   that the physician has the right to request a hearing on the proposed action,

(ii) any time limit (of not less than 30 days) within which to request such a hearing, and

(C) a summary of the rights in the hearing under paragraph (3).

---

[8]   42 U.S.C.§ 11112.

[9]   *Id.*

(2) Notice of hearing. If a hearing is requested on a timely basis under paragraph (1)(B), the physician involved must be given notice stating—

(A) the place, time, and date of the hearing, which date shall not be less than 30 days after the date of the notice, and

(B) a list of the witnesses (if any) expected to testify at the hearing on behalf of the professional review body.

(3) Conduct of hearing and notice. If a hearing is requested on a timely basis under paragraph (1)(B)—

(A) subject to subparagraph (B), the hearing shall be held (as determined by the healthcare entity)—

(i) before an arbitrator mutually acceptable to the physician and the healthcare entity,

(ii) before a hearing officer who is appointed by the entity and who is not in direct economic competition with the physician involved, or

(iii) before a panel of individuals who are appointed by the entity and are not in direct economic competition with the physician involved;

(B) the right to the hearing may be forfeited if the physician fails, without good cause, to appear;

(C) in the hearing the physician involved has the right—

(i) to representation by an attorney or other person of the physician's choice,

(ii) to have a record made of the proceedings, copies of which may be obtained by the physician upon payment of any reasonable charges associated with the preparation thereof,

(iii) to call, examine, and cross-examine witnesses,

(iv) to present evidence determined to be relevant by the hearing officer, regardless of its admissibility in a court of law, and

(v) to submit a written statement at the close of the hearing; and

(D) upon completion of the hearing, the physician involved has the right—

(i) to receive the written recommendation of the arbitrator, officer, or panel, including a statement of the basis for the recommendations, and

(ii) to receive a written decision of the health care entity, including a statement of the basis for the decision.

These requirements apply only to the presumption, and a failure to meet the conditions does not defeat immunity.

2.2.2   What If State Law or the Bylaws Mandate a Different Procedure?

Because HCQIA provides immunity if minimum due process procedures are followed, it is irrelevant whether a hospital followed its own procedures as set forth in the medical staff bylaws, or as required by state law:

> HCQIA immunity is not coextensive with compliance with an in-dividual hospital's bylaws. Rather, the statute imposes a uniform set of national standards. Provided that a peer review action as defined by the statute complies with those standards, a failure to comply with hospital bylaws does not defeat a peer reviewer's right to HCQIA immunity from damages. It bears emphasizing that this does not mean that hospitals and peer review commit-tees that comply with the HCQIA's requirements are free to violate the applicable bylaws and state law. HCQIA does not gainsay the potential for abuse of the peer review process. To the contrary, Congress limited the reach of immunity to money damages. The doors to the courts remain open to doctors who are subjected to unjustified or malicious peer review, and they may seek appropri-ate injunctive and declaratory relief in response to such treatment.[10]

The converse, however, is also true. HCQIA immunity does not attach automatically if a hospital follows its bylaws. For example, in *Peper v. St. Mary's Hosp. & Med. Ctr.*,[11] a hospital argued that it was entitled to immu-nity because under the bylaws, which each applicant agreed to follow and be bound by when applying for medical staff membership and clinical privileges, applicants waived their right to a hearing. The court held that regardless of any purported waiver, to be entitled to HCQIA immunity, a practitioner must be

---

[10]   Poliner v. Texas Health Sys., 537 F.3d 368, 380 (5th Cir. 2008). *See also* Meyers v. Columbia/HCA Healthcare Corp., 341 F.3d 461, 469–70 (6th Cir. 2003) (hospital entitled to HCQIA immunity "even assuming [it] did violate the bylaws, [because] the notice and procedures provided complied with the HCQIA's statutory 'safe harbor'); Bakare v. Pinnacle Health Hospitals, Inc., 469 F. Supp. 2d 272, 290 n.33 (M.D. Pa. 2006) ("immunity attaches when the reviewing body satisfies the requirements *under HCQIA*, regardless of its own policies and procedures.") (emphasis in original).

[11]   207 P.3d 881 (Colo. App. 2008).

afforded certain due process. A blanket provision that sought waiver of all due process rights would not be enforced as it was contrary to the spirit of HCQIA:

> Defendants rely on the HCQIA provision making immunity available where procedural "conditions are met (or are waived voluntarily by the physician)," 42 U.S.C. § 11112(b). **They argue Dr. Peper waived his HCQIA procedural rights when he agreed in applying for provisional hospital privileges to be bound by bylaws that provided no hearing rights to provisional staff.** The medical staff bylaw relied on by defendants provides: "Any redelineation of clinical privileges or other adverse action affecting a provisional member does not give rise to the hearing and appeal rights set forth in these Bylaws." Even assuming this provision is consistent with all other applicable bylaws, we hold it was insufficient as a matter of law to waive HCQIA rights.[12]

2.2.3   What Is Immunized?

It is important to note that HCQIA provides only a protection against damages, and does not provide a general immunity to peer review participants. The statute itself provides:

> (a) In general.
>
> (1) Limitation on damages for professional review actions. If a professional review action (as defined in section 431(9) of a professional review body meets all the standards specified in section 412(a). . . .
>
> shall not be liable in damages under any law of the United States or of any State (or political subdivision thereof) with respect to the action. The preceding sentence shall not apply to damages under any law of the United States or any State relating to the civil rights of any person or persons, including the Civil Rights Act of 1964, 42 U.S.C. 2000e, et seq. and the Civil Rights Acts, 42 U.S.C. 1981, et seq. . . .[13]

Accordingly, HCQIA is not really an immunity statute preventing suit. Thus, even if the immunity standards are met, HCQIA will not serve as a basis to dismiss a lawsuit. In many cases, a physician challenging a peer review proceeding will request, in addition to monetary relief, some form of injunc-

---

[12] *Id.* at 888 (emphasis added).
[13] 42 U.S.C. § 11111.

tive relief such as reinstatement to the medical staff. Therefore, regardless of whether a physician may prevail in a suit for damages, the physician may still pursue a claim for injunctive relief.[14]

In addition, immunity applies only to professional review actions— actions based on competency or professional conduct. These are defined as:

> an action or recommendation of a professional review body which is taken or made in the conduct of professional review activity, which is based on the competence or professional conduct of an individual physician (which conduct affects or could affect adversely the health or welfare of a patient or patients), and which affects (or may affect) adversely the clinical privileges, or membership in a professional society, of the physician.[15]

Thus, for the protection to apply, the action must pertain to the clinical privileges of a physician and must be based on the competence or professional conduct of the physician. HCQIA further excludes the following from the definition of professional conduct.

> (A) the physician's association, or lack of association, with a professional society or association,
>
> (B) the physician's fees or the physician's advertising or engaging in other competitive acts intended to solicit or retain business,
>
> (C) the physician's participation in prepaid group health plans, salaried employment, or any other manner of delivering health services whether on a fee-for-service or other basis,
>
> (D) a physician's association with, supervision of, delegation of authority to, support for, training of, or participation in a private group practice with, a member or members of a particular class of health care practitioner or professional, or
>
> (E) any other matter that does not relate to the competence or professional conduct of a physician.[16]

The HCQIA standard, however, is an objective one that looks not at the subjective motives of the actors, but whether reasonable persons, viewing the matter before them, would have concluded that a professional review action was necessary. Furthermore, the exceptions are likewise viewed objectively, and whether the physician believes himself or herself to have been

---

[14] *See, e.g.,* Gordon v. Lewistown Hospital, 423 F.3d 184 (3d Cir. 2005).

[15] 42 U.S.C. § 11151.

[16] *Id.*

disciplined for an improper reason prevents summary judgment if the action was objectively reasonable.[17]

2.2.4   Who Is Immunized Under HCQIA?

HCQIA provides broad immunity to facilities, and individuals acting on behalf of facilities, when conducting peer review activities. The following are delineated as immunized:

- the professional review body,
- any person acting as a member or staff to the body,
- any person under a contract or other formal agreement with the body, and
- any person who participates with or assists the body with respect to the action.

Moreover, HCQIA provides a broad immunity to individuals who provide information to peer review bodies. The statute provides:

> Protection for those providing information to professional review bodies. Notwithstanding any other provision of law, no person (whether as a witness or otherwise) providing information to a professional review body regarding the competence or professional conduct of a physician shall be held, by reason of having provided such information, to be liable in damages under any law of the United States or of any State (or political subdivision thereof) unless such information is false and the person providing it knew that such information was false.[18]

2.3   A STAFF PHYSICIAN IS DISCIPLINED BY MEDICAL STAFF MEMBERS WHO COMPETE WITH THE PHYSICIAN. WHAT CAN BE DONE TO LIMIT POTENTIAL ANTITRUST LIABILITY?

In many hospitals, especially those in rural areas, it is inevitable that competing physicians will be required to review the care provided by a competitor colleague. If there are substantial issues of poor clinical performance or behavioral issues that result in corrective action, allegations of

---

[17]   *See, e.g.,* 423 F.3d at 206.

[18]   42 U.S.C. § 11111(a)(2).

anticompetitive conduct commonly follow. The best practice is to limit the competitor-physician's involvement to the greatest extent possible.

Competitor participation in the peer review process raises two primary issues: (1) Was the competitor acting for his or her own personal gain,[19] and (2) do the protections of HCQIA apply. As addressed in Question 2 above, HCQIA has been interpreted to require an objective standard of reasonableness when evaluating professional review actions. Individual bias or even anticompetitive purpose should not result in liability *provided* the professional review action was objectively reasonable. This was the issue in *Mathews v. Lancaster General Hospital*, where the plaintiff-orthopedic surgeon alleged that his competitors were motivated in the peer review process to oust their rival. As such, the plaintiff argued that the hospital did not terminate his privileges in the "reasonable belief" that doing so promoted quality healthcare.[20]

The Third Circuit rejected these arguments and affirmed summary judgment to the hospitals on HCQIA immunity grounds. Two factors stand out. First, the hospital in *Mathews* retained an independent physician to review the plaintiff's chart, whose review corroborated the initial findings of the plaintiff's competitors. Second, the hospital board made the actual decision to take corrective action against the plaintiff, and there was no evidence that the board acted with any anticompetitive intent. Thus, the Third Circuit affirmed the granting of summary judgment to the hospitals on HCQIA immunity grounds.

The Fourth Circuit in *Oksanen v. Page Mem'l Hosp* rejected similar arguments that competitors in the peer review process were motivated by their own economic gain.[21] There, the plaintiff argued that certain members of the committees had an independent personal stake as they stood to gain financially by removal of the plaintiff from the staff and, thereby, were capable of conspiring with the hospital for purposes of Section 1 of the Sherman Act. As with *Mathews*, a critical factor to the court's decision was that the competitors were not actual decision makers, and, therefore, their opinions were only recommendations.

In sum, individuals who are the targets of peer review proceedings often challenge the results of those proceedings in court and increasingly allege antitrust violations based on the involvement of competitors in the peer review process.

---

[19]   *See,* Question 1 above regarding the Independent Personal Stake Exception.
[20]   87 F.3d 624, 634–35 (3d Cir. 1996).
[21]   945 F.2d 696 (4th Cir. 1991). *cert. denied,* 502 U.S. 1074 (1992). *Compare* Bolt v. Halifax Hosp. Medical Center, 851 F.2d 1273, 1280 (11th Cir. 1988) (hospital and individual members of the medical staff are separate actors who can conspire for purposes of Section 1).

The following guidelines may therefore be helpful in minimizing potential antitrust exposure.

- Any real or potential conflict should be disclosed to the hospital prior to initiating an investigation. When possible, individuals with a conflicting interest should be excluded from the investigation.
- In considering a potential conflict of interest, a hospital and peer review committee should look beyond the specialties of the physicians involved and examine other direct and indirect potential conflicts such as:
  - Financial interests through joint ventures (proposed or developed) between the hospital and other physicians that may give rise to a claim of potential conflict.
  - Potential conflicts of family members, such as a spouse or other relative who may benefit from any action to exclude the physician.
- Where possible, and in situations when a conflict cannot be avoided, the role of the conflicted individual should be relegated to an investigative role designed to provide factual detail, as opposed to ultimate conclusions regarding medical treatment.
- Even in cases where a competing physician is relegated to an investigative role, consider retention of an outside physician to review the care provided by the physician under investigation.
- The board of directors should be actively involved in the decision-making process and should participate actively in reviewing the evidence. This avoids claims that the board acted as a rubber stamp for the decisions made by the medical staff committee.

A related issue is the use of outsider reviewers. Two issues often arise in this context. First, there is a question as to whether the outside reviews are covered by HCQIA immunity. The second issue is whether the reviewer was given a fair opportunity to review the totality of care provided by the physician under investigation.

As to the first issue, HCQIA protects outside consultants acting on behalf of a peer review committee provided there is a formal relationship with the consultant.[22] To demonstrate the formal relationship, the duties of the consultant should be spelled out in writing to avoid a potential loss of HCQIA immunity. In fact, many sophisticated consultants will not provide services unless there is such an agreement, and most will insist that the hospital agree to hold the consultant harmless if the aggrieved physician claims that the

---

[22]   42 U.S.C. § 11111.

process was improper. As an added protection, it is wise to obtain an agreement from the hospital's directors and officers liability insurer so that the consultant is covered under the hospital's insurance policy.

The final issue is what information will be provided to the consultant. This is often a balance between not overwhelming the consultant by seeking review of every case and providing sufficient information from which the consultant can make a reasonable assessment of the care provided by the physician under investigation. In cases where the care involves only one incident and the only question is whether the investigated physician's conduct was within the standard of care, it may be appropriate to provide information relevant to the one case.

In instances where there are a number of cases and the issue is whether, overall, the physician is providing an appropriate level of care, then a wider selection of cases is necessary to make a reasonable assessment. In these situations, the best practice is to allow the outside reviewer to determine a sampling methodology and the number of cases that should be reviewed. A hospital and peer review committee should avoid a situation where it unilaterally selects the cases to be reviewed, as this can lead to a charge that the hospital skewed the sample to include only known bad cases while avoiding cases demonstrating appropriate quality of care. The consultant's conclusions must be limited to the cases reviewed, and such an opinion cannot be used to establish, overall, that the physician's practice did not meet the appropriate level of care. This is not to say that a limited review cannot result in corrective action. To the contrary, if the care provided as evidenced by the cases reviewed demonstrates such a poor level of care that these cases themselves warrant corrective action, HCQIA does not mandate a review of every case. The stated reasons for the corrective action, however, must be limited to the cases reviewed.

2.4   A HOSPITAL AT WHICH PHYSICIANS PRACTICE ENTERS INTO AN EXCLUSIVE CONTRACT FOR ANESTHESIA SERVICES. WHAT ARE THE ANTITRUST ISSUES THESE PHYSICIANS NEED TO WORRY ABOUT?

Exclusive contracts between hospitals and physicians for certain hospital-based services such as anesthesiology, pathology, and radiology have become ubiquitous given the administrative simplicity, care coordination, and standardization they provide as well as the potential to excluded other competitors. Although most exclusive contracts do not raise concerns under the antitrust laws, they are nonetheless a frequent source of litigation and are not free from antitrust risk. It is therefore important to understand the antitrust dynamics at play in exclusive contracts to avoid potential issues and to mount a successful defense if the contract is challenged.

Exclusive contracts are often challenged by unsuccessful provider groups under Sections 1 and 2 of the Sherman Antitrust Act as illegal exclusive dealing cases, group boycotts, and tying arrangements. Accordingly, both the institutional provider (i.e., the hospital) and the services providers (physician groups) are often alleged to have conspired under Section 1. Because the physician group is not acting as a peer review agent for the hospital in these cases, the intra-corporate immunity doctrine does not typically apply. Physicians have also alleged exclusive dealing under Section 2. Briefly, Section 1 prohibits conspiracies in restraint of trade while Section 2 prohibits monopolization, attempts to monopolize, and conspiracies to monopolize.

Exclusive dealing cases are governed by the rule of reason. *Rule of reason analysis* examines whether the defendants have market power and whether the exclusive contract substantially forecloses rivals from competing in the market.[23] Even if there is market power, under the rule of reason balancing test, the defendants may justify the exclusive contract by demonstrating that there are substantial business reasons for the contract. Indeed, many exclusive contracting cases focus on the justifications for the exclusive contract without focusing on the predicate issue of whether anticompetitive effects are present in the first place.

The leading case in the hospital context is *Jefferson Parish Hosp. Dist. No. 2 v. Hyde,*[24] which involved a challenge to an exclusive contract for anesthesiology services. The exclusive contract barred the plaintiff, a rival anesthesiologist, from providing services at the hospital. The Court held that any anticompetitive effects created by the policy of exclusivity were offset by the hospital's interest in providing efficient and effective healthcare services to its patients. The reasoning here is that such contracts are easier to administer and may promote increased quality of care through standardization.

2.4.1   Issues of Dual Market Definition: National Job Market and Local Patient Market

Although issues of product market definition do not often play a central role in antitrust cases in the staff privilege context, they are a key component in exclusive contracting cases. In cases where excluded physicians challenge

---

[23] Jefferson Parish Hospital Dist. No. 2 v. Hyde, 466 U.S. 2 (1984), amended on other grounds by Illinois Tool Works Inc. v. Independent Ink, Inc. 547 U.S. 28 (2006) (antitrust patent issues).

[24] 466 U.S. 2 (1984).

exclusive contracts, many courts have examined the contract's competitive effects in two markets: The job market for physicians and the market for patient services. In many instances, this market for physician jobs is national, thereby warranting dismissal of many of these types of claims for lack of anticompetitive effects. Indeed, in *Jefferson Parish*, the Supreme Court noted that the circuit court failed to address this issue:

> While the Court of Appeals did discuss the impact of the contract upon patients, it did not discuss its impact upon anesthesiologists. The District Court had referred to evidence that in the entire State of Louisiana there are 156 anesthesiologists and 345 hospitals with operating rooms. The record does not tell us how many of the hospitals in the New Orleans metropolitan area have "open" anesthesiology departments and how many have closed departments. Respondent, for example, practices with two other anesthesiologists at a hospital which has an open department; he previously practiced for several years in a different New Orleans hospital and, prior to that, had practiced in Florida. The record does not tell us whether there is a shortage or a surplus of anesthesiologists in any part of the country, or whether they are thriving or starving.[25]

Thus, where the market is properly defined as the job market for physicians, and where such positions are available on a national level, the market must properly be delineated as a national market. In such cases, it is very unlikely that a physician challenge to such contracts will be successful because an exclusive contract in one market is unlikely to substantially foreclose the excluded physician from seeking and obtaining employment elsewhere in the nation.[26]

In addition to the market for physician jobs, exclusive contract cases also implicate the patient services market. Indeed, this was the case in *Oltz v. St. Peter's Community Hosp.*,[27] where the court held that exclusive contracts implicate both markets because individual patients had a preference for particular anesthesiologists. Thus, the markets in exclusive contracting cases are often analyzed from both a patient perspective and a physician perspective. If the exclusive contract works no substantial foreclosure in either market and only involves the shuffling of competitors in the markets, then the contract is unlikely to have anticompetitive effects.[28]

---

[25] 466 U.S. at 8 n.6.

[26] Collins v. Associated Pathologists, Ltd., 844 F.2d 473 (7th Cir. 1988)

[27] 861 F.2d 1440, 1447 (9th Cir. 1988).

[28] Balalaw v. Lovell, 14 F.3d 793 (2d Cir. 1994).

2.4.2   Efficiency and Business Justifications

A central component in the *Jefferson Parish* decision was the hospital's efficiency justifications for entering into the exclusive contract. In this regard, the hospital was able to establish that there were legitimate quality of care reasons for the exclusive contract in terms of ease of scheduling, ensuring anesthesiology coverage, and maintaining quality.[29]

Courts have also recognized that a hospital has a legitimate interest in protecting its own investments when it employs physicians. In *Four Corners Nephrology Assoc. v. Bevan*,[30] for example, the court held that a hospital was justified in entering into an exclusive contract with a nephrologist it recruited because it had expended money to employ a nephrologist to practice in the community. Under the facts of the case, the hospital argued that by entering into an exclusive contract with the employed physician, it was protecting its interest in the physician. It argued that allowing another physician to practice would result in a diminution of income to the hospital. The court agreed and granted summary judgment to the hospital.

Therefore, although exclusive contracts typically do not present sig-nificant antitrust risks, they are a frequent source of litigation, especially (1) when a facility is moving from an open staff model—where all physicians with privileges could provide the services—to an exclusive arrangement, and (2) in situations where one physician or physician group is being replaced by a competitor. Nevertheless, a hospital considering implementing an exclusive contract may want to think about the following risk management strategies:

- Appoint a board-level committee to determine the potential efficien-cies to be generated by an exclusive agreement. While this is not mandatory under the antitrust laws, it can help to show that there were legitimate grounds for entering into such a contract and can be particularly helpful in situations where a facility is moving from an open staff model to an exclusive contracting model.

- If the decision to enter into an exclusive contract is based on business reasons, the facility should make all attempts to avoid having poten-tial bidders involved in the decision-making process. The facility can and should, however, solicit the opinions of users of the services in question to determine their views on the potential efficiencies. This evidence could be helpful if the contract is challenged.

- A fair opportunity to bid should be provided to all interested groups, and each proposal should be evaluated fairly. The facility may also

---

[29]   466 U.S. at 24 n.42.

[30]   2009 U.S. App. LEXIS 21320 (10th Cir. 2009).

want to consider advertising in relevant national journals to the extent that groups/individuals outside of the area are potentially interested in bidding on the exclusive contract.

- Although not an antitrust issue, a facility should evaluate its bylaws and other credentialing documents to determine the effect of the exclusive contract on individuals currently credentialed to provide the services covered by the exclusive contract.

2.5   DO STATE LAW PEER REVIEW PRIVILEGE LAWS APPLY IN FEDERAL ANTITRUST CASES?

State law peer review privilege laws do not apply in federal antitrust cases where federal law provides the rule of decision. First, there is no federal peer review protection privilege. In *University of Pennsylvania v. EEOC*,[31] the Supreme Court held that neither federal common law nor the First Amendment warranted the recognition of a privilege for a University's academic peer review materials. Therefore, as a general rule, because most antitrust claims are brought in federal court based on federal antitrust law, the state law peer review privilege will not apply.

Although some physicians and hospitals have argued that peer review materials are protected by the HCQIA of 1986, these arguments have likewise failed. Courts are extremely hesitant to recognize a privilege in areas where—as here—it appears that Congress has considered the relevant competing concerns but has declined to provide the privilege itself.[32] According to courts addressing the issue, "Congress has addressed the confidentiality of medical peer review materials in [HCQIA] and has concluded that those [materials] do not warrant protection."[33]

Additionally, some providers have attempted to argue that if a complaint contains both federal claims and ancillary state law claims, the state's peer review privilege should apply. This argument, however, has been rejected, as federal law governs the assertion of a privilege where jurisdiction is based on the existence of a federal question.[34] Nevertheless, a state law peer review

---

[31]   493 U.S. 182, 110 S. Ct. 577, 107 L. Ed. 2d 571 (1990).

[32]   *Id.* at 189 (cautioning that courts should be "especially reluctant to recognize a privilege in an area where it appears that Congress has considered the relevant competing concerns but has not provided the privilege itself").

[33]   Doe v. Smith, 2000 U.S. Dist. LEXIS 22322, *6 (E.D. N.Y.). *See also,* Syposs, 63 F. Supp. 2d at 307 W.D.N.Y. 1999); Johnson, 169 F.R.D. at 560–61 and n.15 (discussing HCQIA's legislative history).

[34]   Memorial Hospital for McHenry County v. Shadur, 664 F.2d 1058, 1061 n.3 (7th Cir. 1981).

privilege may apply to a complaint in federal court based solely on a state law cause of action.[35]

2.6   ARE GOVERNMENTAL HOSPITALS TREATED ANY DIFFERENTLY FROM PRIVATE HOSPITALS UNDER THE ANTITRUST LAWS?

Governmental hospitals, such as state and county hospitals, may have additional defenses available to them that are not available to private hospitals, such as the State Action Doctrine and immunity under the Local Government Antitrust Act.

The State Action Doctrine exempts from liability anticompetitive conduct that is authorized by the state. Governmental hospitals will often argue, in the privileging context, that because they are authorized to credential physicians, it is foreseeable that some physicians will be excluded from the medical staff.[36] Typically, a municipal hospital must show that its conduct is derived from a clearly articulated state policy. This is interpreted to mean that the anticompetitive conduct is a foreseeable result of the policy.[37] Additionally, the activities of private physicians who are working on behalf of a state hospital may also be immune. Nevertheless, to be entitled to immunity, private parties must have their actions "actively supervised" by the state. This means that the state must play some actual role in the process, for example, by engaging in rate setting. Mere passive supervision is not enough.

In *LaFaro v. New York Cardiothoracic Group, PLLC*,[38] for example, the issue was whether two private cardiothoracic surgeons who maintained privileges at a county facility were improperly excluded from practicing there after the hospital entered into an exclusive contract with another group. As to the hospital, it held that a finding of immunity was warranted because the hospital was created by the legislature for the express purpose of operating a hospital, and any anticompetitive behavior by it—including exclusive contracting— was a foreseeable consequence of this authorization. As a result, the conduct

---

[35]   Bredice v. Doctor's Hospital, 50 F.R.D. 249 (D. D. C. 1970); Weekoty v. United States, 30 F. Supp. 2d 1343 (D. N. M. 1998).

[36]   California Retail Liquor Dealers Assn. v. Midcal Aluminum, Inc., 445 U.S. 97 (1980); Town of Hallie v. City of Eau Claire, 471 U.S. 34, 44 (1985).

[37]   471 U.S. 47.

[38]   570 F.3d 471 (2d Cir. 2009). *Compare* Stratienko v. Chattanooga-Hamilton County Hospital, 2009 WL 736007 (E.D. Tenn. 2009) (privately employed physicians who were serving on the hospital's medical executive committee were immune under the state action doctrine as they were acting as agents of the hospital regarding the discipline of the plaintiff).

met the clearly articulated requirement of the test. The court held that there were insufficient facts to determine whether the private physicians met the active supervision prong of the State Action Doctrine. Nevertheless, the court left open the question of whether the hospital could be held liable under the antitrust laws for any unsupervised conduct engaged in by the private defendants. As to the physician defendants, the court rejected the argument proffered by them that they did not need to establish active supervision because they were acting pursuant to a contract with a state hospital.

The Local Government Antitrust Act immunizes local governments from damages or attorney's fees:

> No damages, interest on damages, costs, or attorney's fees may be recovered under section 4, 4A, or 4C of the Clayton Act (15 U.S.C. 15, 15a, or 15c) from any local government, or official or employee thereof acting in an official capacity.[39]

Similarly, officials and those acting under the direction of a local government are also immunized:

> No damages, interest on damages, costs, or attorney's fees may be recovered under section 4, 4A, or 4C of the Clayton Act (15 U.S.C. 15, 15a, or 15c) from any local government, or official or employee thereof acting in an official capacity.[40]

2.7   WHAT ARE THE ANTITRUST IMPLICATIONS OF ECONOMIC CREDENTIALING POLICIES?

Economic credentialing is a generic term that connotes many different types of policies and practices. In its simplest form, economic credentialing occurs when medical staff membership or clinical privileges are awarded to a physician or other licensed independent practitioner based on factors that are not related directly to clinical competency or professional conduct.[41] These factors often include, but are not limited to, the business/economic goals of the hospital, utilization of hospital resources by staff physicians, and whether the physician competes with the hospital or is affiliated with a competing facility. Economic credentialing differs from traditional medical staff

---

[39]   15 U.S.C. § 35.

[40]   15 U.S.C. § 36(a). *See also* Sandcrest Outpatient Services, P.A. v. Cumberland County Hospital System, Inc., 853 F.2d 1139 (4th Cir. 1988) (director and chief of staff were immunized from damages under LGAA).

[41]   American Medical Association, Policy H230.975, www.ama-assn.org/ama1/pub/upload/mm/475/811.doc (last visited Feb. 9, 2009) (economic credentialing).

credentialing in that the considerations are not based primarily on quality of care, competency, or professional conduct.

Although there are numerous types of economic credentialing policies, conflict-of-interest policies typically create the most antitrust controversy. A typical conflict-of-interest policy mandates the denial of medical staff membership or certain clinical privileges to physicians who, directly or indirectly, acquire or maintain an ownership or investment interest in a facility that competes with the acute care hospital. Conflict-of-interest policies may be broadly defined; in *Baptist Health v. Murphy*,[42] for example, the hospital defined direct ownership as an ownership interest by the practitioner or the practitioner's immediate family.

Conflict-of-interest policies reflect the growing competition between hospitals and physicians who own ambulatory surgery centers (ASCs), specialty hospitals, or other facilities that compete with the services offered by acute care hospitals. They reflect the perception of many acute care hospitals that physicians are "cream-skimming" the most profitable commercially-insured patients for their own financial benefit while leaving less profitable patients to the hospitals, thereby threatening the hospitals' financial health.

Individuals and entities affected by economic credentialing policies will often allege that there is an improper restraint of trade under Section 1 of the Sherman Act, or that the hospital has monopolized, or is attempting to monopolize, the market for the particular service under Section 2 of the Sherman Antitrust Act. Usually, the investor challenges not only the policy, but also related hospital conduct such as attempts by the hospital to exclude the competing center from the market with boycotts and exclusive contracts with payers. The related conduct often has the greatest antitrust significance.

2.7.1   Is the Policy Concerted Activity or Unilateral?

The first issue that must be resolved is whether the conduct is unilateral or joint. *Concerted action*—an agreement by and among separate economic entities—raises greater antitrust concerns than unilateral conduct because it can result in *per se* liability. As the Department of Justice and Federal Trade Commission explained in their *Report on the Health Care Industry,* concerted action raises more serious antitrust concerns in terms of economic credentialing policies because:

> Generally speaking, antitrust law does not limit individual hospitals from unilaterally responding to competition either by terminating physician admitting privileges or by approaching state governments in connection with CON proceedings. If there is specific

---

[42]   226 S.W.3d 800 (Ark. 2006) (granting preliminary injunction to prevent implementation of conflict criteria).

evidence of anticompetitive conduct by individual hospitals or of hospitals colluding together against efforts to open a Single Specialty Hospital [SSH] or Ambulatory Surgery Center [ASC], then the Agencies will aggressively pursue those activities.[43]

A physician who is threatened with having his or her privileges revoked as the result of a conflict-of-interest policy may potentially challenge the termination under Section 1 of the Sherman Act. If the medical staff is involved in creating or enforcing the economic credentialing policy, such involvement may create more serious challenges under Section 1 because it may implicate concerted action by and among the hospital and medical staff.[44] As a result, hospitals adopting economic conflict-of-interest policies need to be mindful of this difference. Therefore, it is important that the hospital carry out the decision to adopt economic criteria in a unilateral manner, and the medical staff should not be involved in the creation of such policies. Although this is usually the case, given the politically charged nature of such policies, there are potential pitfalls that can place seemingly unilateral conduct under the auspices of Section 1. This includes situations where the medical staff is involved in creating or enforcing the criteria even though the hospital has the ultimate decision-making authority.

Most claims challenging economic credentialing policies are brought under Section 2 of the Sherman Act that prohibits the illegal formation or maintenance of monopolies. Section 2 does not require concerted action. Nevertheless, monopoly power under Section 2 is more difficult to establish than market power under Section 1.[45] Typical Section 2 theories applied in the economic credentialing context include attempts to monopolize, refusals to deal, and allegations that a hospital is engaged in predatory exclusionary contracting practices with payers to drive the plaintiff from the market.[46] These strategies are often employed in addition to, and in conjunction with, the creation of conflict-of-interest policies.

---

[43]   Department of Justice and Federal Trade Commission, *Improving Health Care: A Dose of Competition* (2004).

[44]   15 U.S.C. § 1.

[45]   Reazin v. Blue Cross & Blue Shield, Inc., 899 F.2d 951, 966-67 (10th Cir. 1990).

[46]   For example, in Surgical Care Ctr. of Hammond, L.C. v. Hospital Service District No. 1, 309 F.3d 836 (5th Cir. 2002), the plaintiff outpatient surgical facility argued that a hospital attempted to monopolize the outpatient surgical market by entering into exclusive contracts with managed care organizations, and offering steep discounts if the organizations used the hospital's outpatient services instead of the plaintiff's facility.

2.7.2   Are Exclusive Contracts Predatory Conduct?

Challenges to economic conflict-of-interest policies and exclusive contracts have had mixed success. In several instances, courts have dismissed the excluded plaintiff's allegations on threshold issues without examining the merits of the conduct. In *Little Rock Cardiology Clinic v. Baptist Health,*[47] for example, the court granted the defendants' motions to dismiss because the plaintiff failed to allege an appropriate relevant market. The plaintiff cardiologists were investors in a specialty heart hospital that competed with Baptist Health, a dominant hospital. The defendants were Baptist Health and Blue Cross Blue Shield of Arkansas.

The case initially began as a state court proceeding when the plaintiffs challenged an economic credentialing policy adopted by the hospital that had the effect of preventing a physician from maintaining staff privileges at the hospital if that physician maintained a financial interest in a facility that competed with the hospital. The state court enjoined enforcement of the policy, and the plaintiffs subsequently filed a complaint in federal court alleging violations of Sections 1 and 2 of the Sherman Antitrust Act.

In the federal complaint, the plaintiffs alleged that the hospital reacted to the threat of competition from the plaintiffs' specialty heart hospital by conspiring with the insurer to exclude the plaintiff from a popular preferred provider network.[48] The trial court granted the hospital's motion to dismiss because plaintiffs failed to allege a properly defined relevant market in which to assess competitive effects. The plaintiffs contended that the market was for "cardiology procedures obtained in hospitals by patients covered by private insurance."[49] According to the court, the plaintiffs improperly conflated the physician services market, in which the plaintiffs competed, with the market for hospital services in which the plaintiffs did not compete.[50] The court had similar issues with the alleged geographic market, holding that limiting the markets to the cities of Little Rock and North Little Rock was fundamentally implausible. Noting that after two years the plaintiffs set forth "no hint of a

---

[47]   573 F. Supp. 2d 1125 (E.D. Ark. 2008), *aff'd,* 591 F.3d 591 (8th Cir. 2009), *cert. denied,* 2010 U.S. LEXIS 5435 (2010).

[48]   *See* Plaintiffs' Memorandum of Law In Response to Motion to Dismiss Third Amended Complaint at 24, Little Rock Cardiology Clinic v. Baptist Health, 573 F. Supp. 2d 1125 (E.D. Ark. 2005).

[49]   573 F. Supp. 2d at 1142.

[50]   *Id.* at 1146. Additionally, the court took issue with plaintiffs, allegation that a market can be defined by reference to whether the patients were privately insured, as how a purchaser pays for the services was deemed irrelevant to whether the product or services is interchangeable. *Id.* at 1147.

Healthcare Antitrust FAQ Handbook, First Edition

coherent and promising antitrust claim," the court dismissed the complaint with prejudice.[51] The Eighth Circuit affirmed on appeal.

In other matters, courts have allowed the claims to proceed to trial. Similar allegations were made in *Heartland Surgical Specialty Hospital, LLC v. Midwest Division, Inc.*[52] There, the plaintiff, a physician-owned specialty hospital providing orthopedic, neurological, plastic, general surgery, and pain management services, filed an antitrust suit against a number of hospitals, including HCA, and a number of other managed care organizations including Aetna Health Care and Coventry.[53] The plaintiff claimed that the defendant hospitals conspired with the managed care organizations to prevent it from obtaining necessary managed care contracts and access to a sufficient volume of commercially insured patients. Without such contracts, it argued that it could not effectively compete.[54]

A central focus of the dispute was a "network configuration" clause contained in the managed care contracts requiring that the managed care organization obtain the approval of the contracted hospital before allowing a new facility into the network.[55] The provision automatically increased HCA's reimbursement by 10 percent in the event that a managed care organization included a new facility on its panel without HCA's consent.[56] No real justification was proffered by HCA for the provision, and it was intended as "punitive" if Coventry admitted "niche" providers into the network. Finding sufficient issues of fact to deny summary judgment, such as dinners hosted by one of the hospitals where the topic of competition with specialty hospitals was discussed,[57] the court allowed the antitrust claims to proceed to trial.

2.7.3 Can the Coercion of Physicians Be Deemed Predatory Conduct?

Allegations of coercion are made frequently in cases where physicians have opened competing clinics and contend that the hospital has engaged in

---

[51]   *Id.* at 1152 (quoting E. Food Servs., Inc. v. Pontifical Catholic Univ. Serv. Ass'n Inc., 357 F.3d 1, 9 (1st Cir. 2004).

[52]   527 F. Supp. 2d 1257 (D. Kan. 2007).

[53]   United, Cigna, Blue Cross, Humana, and North Kansas City Hospital settled with the plaintiff and were dismissed from the case. *Id.* at 1263.

[54]   *Id.* at 1264.

[55]   *Id.* at 1269.

[56]   *Id.* at 1271.

[57]   *Id.* at 1288–89.

predatory acts to prevent physicians from referring to the competing center.[58] These can take the form of alleged intimidation of referral sources as well as through the use of conflict-of-interest policies that some courts have found to be evidence of predatory conduct.

One of the leading cases in this context is *Rome Ambulatory Surgical Center v. Rome Memorial Hospital.*[59] The plaintiff, Rome Ambulatory Surgical Center, was a physician-owned ambulatory surgery center that filed an antitrust action against a hospital contending that the hospital conspired to drive it out of the market for ambulatory surgery services in Rome, New York. Among other things, the center contended that the hospital engaged in a pattern of anticompetitive activity designed to prevent competition by entering into exclusive contracts with health plans, intimidating surgeons who desired to use the surgery center, threatening to withhold privileges from physicians who used the center, and inducing a group of physicians to refer exclusively to the defendant hospital.[60] The plaintiff alleged that the defendant hospital foreclosed a large percentage of the insured outpatient surgery market, such that it denied the plaintiff the opportunity to compete. Denying the defendants' motion for summary judgment, the court rejected the hospital's argument that it was merely protecting its turf and found sufficient evidence of predatory conduct to proceed to trial.[61] The court denied the defendant's motion to dismiss the exclusive contracting and monopolization claims, finding sufficient predatory conduct in terms of the hospital's intimidation of referral sources and utilization of exclusive contracts to prevent entry into the market.[62]

The plaintiff also challenged a conflict-of-interest policy contained in the defendant hospital bylaws that allowed the medical staff to consider "the nature and extent of ownership . . . interest held by the applicant . . . in any health care facility which is in direct competition with the hospital" when determining whether to grant staff privileges to a physician. The hospital defended its conduct on the grounds that the plaintiff-investor physicians used the competing facility to refer profitable procedures to their facility,

---

[58] *See, e.g.,* Gordon v. Lewistown Hosp., 423 F.3d 184 (3d Cir. 2005); Imaging Ctr., Inc. v. W. Md. Health Sys., Inc., 2004-2 Trade Cases (CCH) ¶ 74,566 (D. Md. 2004) (plaintiff claimed that hospital coerced its physicians not to refer to center, and to that end, tracked physician referrals to competing centers). *Compare* Defiance Hosp., Inc. v. Fauster-Cameron, Inc., 344 F. Supp. 2d 1097 (N.D. Ohio 2004) (Section 2 suit by hospital alleging that clinic operated by physicians attempted to monopolize anesthesia market to prevent competition by hospital. Clinic refused to provide anesthesia coverage by CRNAs to hospital).

[59] 349 F. Supp. 2d 389 (N.D.N.Y. 2004).

[60] *Id.* at 397.

[61] *Id.* at 410–11.

[62] *Id.* at 417.

while steering unprofitable cases to the hospital. Although the hospital never utilized the bylaw provision, the court held that the threat could be viewed as predatory.[63]

2.8 BUSINESS JUSTIFICATIONS FOR ECONOMIC CREDENTIALING: PROTECTING AGAINST FREE-RIDING

Acute care hospitals will often argue that economic credentialing policies are necessary to prevent free-riding. They charge that physicians are diverting high-reimbursement patients to their own facilities and leaving unprofitable patients to the hospital, which cannot refuse to treat a patient on the basis of reimbursement. This alleged ability of physicians to divert unprofitable patients to the hospital is a form of free-riding.

Preventing free-riding is a well-established economic justification for seemingly anticompetitive conduct under the antitrust laws and appears in a number of contexts.[64] In summary, the defense is invoked where a firm creates a policy to prevent a competitor from benefiting from its work. The doctrine has not been explicitly offered as a defense in any reported healthcare antitrust cases. Rather, it has been invoked primarily in manufacturer/dealer cases.

A classic expression of the rationale to prevent free-riding can be found in *Continental T.V., Inc. v. GTE Sylvania, Inc.*[65] The United States Supreme Court held that a geographic requirement prohibiting its franchised retailers from selling Sylvania televisions outside of their franchised area was appropriate because such restrictions promoted interbrand competition by allowing the manufacturer to obtain efficiencies in distribution and prevented potential free-riding by discount dealers. [66]

The doctrine is designed to prevent one competitor from taking unfair advantage of the work of another competitor. The focus is on prevention of unfair competition, where one competitor benefits by obtaining a service from the other for which it does not have to pay. In the economic credentialing context, hospitals often argue that the perceived ability by physicians to "preselect" favorable patients puts the hospital at an unfair economic advantage. Acute care hospitals contend that smaller specialty hospitals are better able to

---

[63] *Id.* at 422. The conspiracy to monopolize claim also survived summary judgment. The case was settled before trial.

[64] A more comprehensive treatment of this defense may be found in M. Mattioli, *Can Preventing Diversion of Profitable Patients Justify Hospitals' Economic Credentialing under the Antitrust Laws?*, 1 J. Health & Life Sci. 39 (2008).

[65] 433 U.S. 36 (1977).

[66] *Id.* at 55.

compete on price because (1) an acute care hospital must bear the expense of providing the full panoply of services; and (2) a full-service acute care hospital must accept all patients regardless of ability to pay. If a physician is able to shift the low-reimbursement patients to the hospital, while keeping only the high-reimbursement patients for his or her own facility, the physician is able to benefit from the hospital's inability to preselect patients.

In conclusion, economic credentialing issues often implicate the antitrust laws because they can appear to prohibit competition. Because of the potential anticompetitive arguments that can be made to challenge such policies, they need to be analyzed carefully to determine their full anticompetitive effects. They are not "one size fits all" type policies, and each must be tailored to the specifics of the particular hospital.

3

Healthcare Competition Issues

Alexander M. McIntyre, Jr., Esquire

Baker, Donelson, Bearman, Caldwell & Berkowitz PC

The strategies that hospitals and healthcare providers use to protect and/ or enhance their competitive positions are the focus of this chapter. These strategies may include efforts to exclude other competitors by entering into exclusive contracts with key payers, opposing the certificate of need (CON) of a competitor, and denying a competitor access to the hospital or a needed service.

As with many antitrust issues, the answers to these questions depend, typically, on the market conditions that exist in the area and whether the participants have sufficient market power to affect the competitive landscape. As an overarching issue, the antitrust laws are designed to protect the competitive process and not individual competitors, *per se*. Therefore, practices that affect only one competitor are not usually within the ambit of the antitrust laws because the antitrust laws assume that competitors will fight vigorously to take business from each other. The distinction between vigorous competition and an antitrust violation is dependent on a host of factors that are described in the hypothetical examples below.

3.1 THE LOCAL HOSPITAL ENTERS INTO AN EXCLUSIVE CONTRACT WITH THE PRIMARY PAYER THAT WILL NOT CONTRACT WITH A SURGERY CENTER. IS THIS LEGAL?

The answer, like the answers to so many questions in antitrust, is that it depends on the market and how much of the market will be foreclosed by the particular transaction. For example, if, as is the case in a number of states, a single private payer vastly predominates, a surgery center would presumably not be able to survive for long taking only self-pay and Medicare patients. This would be of little competitive concern if there were a number of in-network surgery centers competing with the hospital such that the exclusion of the shut-out surgery center will not affect whether there are constraints on the hospital's ability to raise rates to supracompetitive levels. However, if the hospital faced little or no competition, an exclusive contract would tend to perpetuate a monopoly and probably be vulnerable to an antitrust challenge.

Similarly, if there are a number of substantial payers serving a particular community, access to one payer's network would not necessarily be critical to the success or failure of the surgery center, and an exclusive agreement might foster lower reimbursement rates in exchange for a guarantee of additional patients. With the surgery center foreclosed from only a relatively small segment of the market, the procompetitive benefits and efficiencies engendered by an exclusive agreement between a payer and a provider would probably outweigh any competitive harm and thus pass antitrust muster.

Ultimately, the proof of anticompetitive effect in a properly defined relevant market is crucial to success or failure of the case. Exclusive dealing cases are analyzed under the rule of reason. This means that the effects of the transaction on the market must be proven. Accordingly, exclusive dealing cases require that the parties analyze the markets being affected by the practice. Thus, an examination as to the amount of the market that is being foreclosed is necessary to determine whether the practice will violate the Sherman Antitrust Act. If, for example, the exclusive arrangement will not foreclose a significant portion of the market, then there are likely no anticompetitive effects. The seminal healthcare case regarding exclusive contracts is *Jefferson Parish Hosp. Dist. No. 2 v. Hyde*.[1] The issue in *Jefferson Parish* was whether an exclusive contract with an anesthesiology group violated the antitrust laws. Analyzing the case under the rule of reason, the Supreme Court held that the plaintiff failed to properly define the market that it determined was the market for anesthesiology contracts. Therefore, analysis of an exclusive contract involves review of the market that is foreclosed to the participants.

As to the amount of foreclosure that must exist, different courts and tribunals have come to different conclusions. The Federal Trade Commission (FTC) found in *In re Toys "R" Us, Inc.*, that the respondent violated the antitrust laws where it used its power as a purchaser of 40 percent of the toy sales to induce manufacturers to refuse to deal with warehouses that competed with Toys "R" Us.[2] Nevertheless, some courts have allowed exclusive contracts to stand where the parties had an 80 percent market share and there were sufficient business justifications for the exclusive contract.[3]

---

[1] 466 U.S. 2 (1984).

[2] 5 Trad Reg. Rptr. (CCH) ¶ 24,516 (FTC 1998), *aff'd* 224 F.3d 928 (7th Cir. 2000).

[3] Barry White Corp. v. ITT Grinnell Corp., 724 F.2d 227 (1st Cir. 1983).

Two recent cases illustrate this in the context of provider/payer exclusivity. First, in *Little Rock Cardiology Clinic, PA v. Baptist Health,*[4] the Eighth Circuit Court of Appeals dismissed antitrust claims against Baptist Health, a full-service hospital in Little Rock, Arkansas, for allegedly conspiring with Blue Cross Blue Shield of Arkansas to exclude a group of cardiologists from the market for "cardiology procedures obtained in hospitals by patients covered by private insurance" in Little Rock. In 1997, the cardiologists opened Arkansas Heart Hospital, a competitor to Baptist, and soon thereafter Blue Cross terminated its network provider agreement with the cardiologists. Moreover, in 2003, Baptist instituted credentialing policies that foreclosed staff privileges to any doctor who held an interest in a competing hospital.[5] The trial court found that the cardiologists failed to plead a plausible relevant market and dismissed their claim, and the appellate court agreed, finding both the doctors' proposed geographic area too limited and the patient market improperly restricted to those with private insurance, rather than to all patients capable of paying for their medical bills.

In contrast, an Illinois federal district court denied summary judgment in favor of St. Francis Medical Center, the largest hospital in Peoria, Illinois, allowing an ambulatory surgery center (ASC), Peoria Day Surgery Center (PDSC), to pursue its antitrust claims.[6] In the 1990s, a predecessor of PDSC contracted with Caterpillar, the largest employer in Peoria, to treat its health plan beneficiaries. Later, St. Francis informed Caterpillar that it wanted to cover the services offered by PDSC. In 2001, Caterpillar agreed to make St. Francis its exclusive provider of ambulatory surgical services if St. Francis could meet Caterpillar's needs. When St. Francis later opened several ASCs, Caterpillar informed PDSC that it was no longer considered in-network for urological surgical facility charges. Without reaching the merits, the Court found that PSDC's expert provided evidence that raised genuine issues of material fact as to whether the exclusive agreement between Caterpillar and St. Francis prevented other ASCs from entering the market, improperly limited patient choices and quality of case, and raised prices. (The case was settled shortly after summary judgment was denied.)

The government, however, may take a different view of exclusive contracts especially where they may be designed to prevent competition. In

---

[4]   591 F.3d 591 (8th Cir. 2009).

[5]   In a separate proceeding in state court, the Arkansas Supreme Court ultimately upheld an injunction against Baptist's economic credentialing policies on the grounds that, inter alia, they improperly inhibited competition and interfered with the doctor-patient relationship. Baptist Health v. Murphy, 2010 Ark. 358 (Sept. 30, 2010).

[6]   Docket No. 06-1236, United States District Court, Central District of Illinois.

United States and State of Texas v. United Regional Health Care System,[7] the Department of Justice and the State of Texas challenged a provider that had entered into exclusive contracts with commercial health insurers that effectively prevented the insurers from contracting with United Regional's competitors. The government alleged that United Regional had unlawfully used those contracts to maintain its monopoly for hospital services in violation of Section 2 of the Sherman Act. The Complaint alleged that United Regional: (i) delayed and prevented the expansion and entry of its competitors, likely leading to higher healthcare costs and higher health insurance premiums; (ii) limited price competition for price-sensitive patients, likely leading to higher healthcare costs for those patients; and (iii) reduced quality competition between United Regional and its competitors. United Regional, it was alleged, maintained a 65 percent market share for commercial payers and was a "must have" hospital for health plans. Plans refusing to offer United Regional an exclusive contract were forced to pay anywhere from 13 percent to 27 percent more for its services. Thus, the government concluded that the arrangements were designed to preserve United Regional's monopoly power in the geographic market.

Exclusionary contracts may be a problem if they (i) foreclose a significant portion of the market and thereby prevent competition or (ii) are used to facilitate a monopoly. Accordingly, the relevant inquiry will be whether other payers are available with which to contract or whether the exclusionary contract ties up a significant portion of the market and thereby prevents competition. Additionally, the market share of the participating parties must be examined to determine whether the exclusive contracting is being used to preserve (or form) a monopoly for the respective services. Absent significant foreclosure or monopoly power, it is unlikely that an exclusive contract on its own will create an antitrust risk. Nevertheless, the competitive markets should be examined to determine whether the agreement will create antitrust risks.

3.2 THE LOCAL HOSPITAL OPPOSES A SURGERY CENTER'S REQUEST FOR A CERTIFICATE OF NEED. IS THIS AN ANTITRUST VIOLATION?

It is unlikely that opposing a competitor's CON would be deemed an antitrust violation as such activity would likely be a form of governmental petitioning and immune from the antitrust laws.[8] Genuine attempts to

---

[7]   Case No.: 7:11-cv-00030 (RCO) (N.D. Tex.), *available at* http://www.justice.gov/atr/cases/unitedregional.html.

[8]   *See* Hospital Building Company v. Trustees of The Rex Hospital, 791 F.2d 288 (4th Cir. 1986).

influence government action are protected from antitrust challenge by the Noerr-Pennington doctrine.[9] This is true even if the motivation is obviously anticompetitive.[10] The Noerr-Pennington doctrine would likewise protect a number of competitors who jointly opposed a CON application. However, if the hospital's opposition to the CON is objectively meritless and maintained solely to impede the surgery center's entry into the market, it could be considered a sham, unprotected by Noerr-Pennington.

Additionally, depending on the CON program of a particular state, the local hospital's opposition may be protected by the state action doctrine, which immunizes activity undertaken pursuant to an articulated state policy to displace competition and also subject to effective governmental review.[11] In enacting CON legislation, the state's legislature has articulated a market allocation policy, and CON applications are typically subject to rigorous scrutiny; thus, both prerequisites for application of the state action doctrine are satisfied.

At the same time, not all action taken by a state agency is protected by the state action doctrine. For example, in July 2010, the FTC filed an administrative complaint against the North Carolina Dental Board alleging that the Board's actions prohibiting non-dentists from offering teeth whitening services violated the antitrust laws. The North Carolina Dental Board consists of six dentists and two non-dentists.[12] The FTC alleged that the Board's activities are not authorized by statute. In refusing to dismiss the complaint and finding that the activity was not immune from antitrust scrutiny, the FTC held that active state supervision was required because the Board is controlled by participants in the market; therefore, without suitable state supervision, the activity was not immune.

Under most circumstances, however, petitioning activity will be immune. It is only when such petitioning becomes a sham that immunity is removed; these circumstances are rare, and even legitimate petitioning that is designed to thwart competition is protected.

---

[9] Eastern R.R. Presidents Conference v. Noerr Motor Freight, Inc., 365 U.S. 127 (1961) and United Mine Workers v. Pennington, 381 U.S. 657 (1965).

[10] *E.g.,* City of Columbia v. Omni Outdoor Advertising, Inc., 499 U.S. 365, 381 (1991).

[11] *See, e.g.,* General Hospitals of Humana, Inc. v. Baptist Medical System, Inc., 1986-1 Trade Cas. (CCH) ¶66996, 1986 WL 935 (E.D. Ark. 1986).

[12] In Re. North Carolina Bd. of Dentistry, Docket No. 9343 (July 14, 2010), *available at* http://www.ftc.gov/os/adjpro/d9343/index.shtm. See also, FTC v. Ticor Title Ins. Co., 504 U.S. 621 (1992).

3.3 MAY A HOSPITAL REFUSE TO DEAL WITH A COMPETING SURGERY CENTER BY REFUSING TO SIGN A TRANSFER AGREEMENT OR PROVIDE OTHER SERVICES?

From an antitrust perspective,[13] whether a hospital must cooperate with another provider is a function of the peculiarities of the individual market. As a threshold issue, it matters greatly whether the hospital is acting unilaterally or in concert with another provider (or, for that matter, with a payer) in refusing to deal with the surgery center. Generally, Section 1 of the Sherman Act prohibits contracts, combinations, and conspiracies to restrain trade, including restraining trade by means of boycott. If the hospital is acting in concert with another provider, such an agreement may be a horizontal combination that violates Section 1 of the Sherman Antitrust Act as two competitors refusing to deal with a third may, depending on the particular circumstances, constitute an illegal boycott.

Unlike Section 1, Section 2 of the Sherman Act prohibits single firm efforts to monopolize or attempt to monopolize a relevant market. If the hospital is acting on its own, whether there are antitrust concerns largely depends on the size and market power of the hospital. If, for example, the hospital is relatively small and there are a number of area hospitals to which the surgery center can turn for similar services, then it is unlikely that there would be significant antitrust implications. However, if the hospital were the only acute care facility geographically available to the surgery center and either had no legitimate business rationale for refusing a relationship or, worse, actually suffered short-term losses from its failure to do business with the surgery center, an argument could be made that the hospital was abusing its monopoly power in an attempt to foreclose a competitor.

The general rule is that a competitor, even a monopolist, has no duty to do business with or to assist a competing concern.[14] If a hospital does have a dominant market share, then business practices that involve short-term economic sacrifice (e.g., less revenue) and are not otherwise explicable could be viewed as undertaking longer-term anticompetitive objectives aimed at

---

[13] There may be state laws and federal regulations not directly related to antitrust concerns that are relevant here. Any such regulation is beyond the scope of this treatment.

[14] *E.g.*, Verizon Communications, Inc. v. The Law Office of Curtis V. Trinko, L.L.P., 540 U.S. 398 (2004).

crippling a competitor, especially if the hospital is abandoning a previously profitable course of dealing.[15]

Another issue is the concept of anticompetitive harm. The antitrust laws are designed to protect the competitive process and not individual competitors. In this regard, it is assumed that participants in the market will compete fiercely with one another to gain a competitive position.[16] This type of activity is encouraged by the antitrust laws.

A similar analysis applies to this situation as is discussed above regarding a competitor's duty to deal with a competitor-rival. A starting point is whether the refusal is designed solely to thwart competition or whether there is a legitimate justification for the refusal. Even if the refusal is based solely on competitive concerns, in the absence of market or monopoly power,[17] there is not likely to be significant competitive effects in the market such that competition in general, as opposed to an individual competitor, is harmed.

3.4 A HOME HEALTH AGENCY DEMANDS ACCESS TO HOSPITAL PATIENTS. MUST THIS DEMAND BE HONORED?

It depends on how much of a properly defined market is foreclosed if access is withheld, the hospital's market power within the market, whether the home health agency has been granted access in the past, and the competitive/business justification for denying access. If, for example, the hospital is the only acute care facility in a large geographic area and accounts for most of the hospital admissions from that area, then it follows that the patients served by that hospital will constitute a large percentage of the market for home health services in a similarly defined area. An agreement with one agency to become the exclusive referral of the hospital, absent legitimate business reasons (quality or price of services, for example), could be improper. Conversely, if

---

[15] *E.g.,* Aspen Skiing Co. v. Aspen Highlands Skiing Corp., 472 U.S. 585, 608 (1985). *See also, e.g.,* Four Corners Nephrology Associates, P.C. v. Mercy Medical Center, 582 F.3d 1216, 1225 (10th Cir. 2009)(no liability where the only hospital in Durango, Colorado, refused to grant privileges to competing nephrologist to "avoid an unprofitable relationship").

[16] *See, e.g.,* Seagood Trading Corp. v. Jerrico, 924 F.2d 1555, 1573 (11th Cir. 1991).

[17] There are no hard rules defining market or monopoly power. A lesser market share is typically needed for claims under Section 1 than to establish monopoly power under Section 2. Although dependent on a variety of factors, such as barriers to entry of new competitors, shares of greater than 55 percent are typically required to create an inference of monopoly power. *See* U.S. v. Dentsply Intern., Inc., 399 F.3d 181, 187 (3d Cir. 2005) (75 percent share sufficient).

the hospital had a number of competitors, restricting access to that hospital's patients might have little effect in the home health market.

A number of cases involved claims by durable medical equipment (DME) providers alleging that the defendant hospitals steered patients to the hospital-affiliated DME companies. A leading case that typifies this type of claim is *Key Enterprises of Delaware, Inc. v. Venice Hospital.*[18] There, the plaintiff DME provider alleged that it was forced from the DME market when the defendants, a hospital and an outside DME provider, formed a joint venture to compete in the DME market in Venice, Florida. According to the facts of the case, the defendant hospital (Venice Hospital) was the largest referrer of DME patients to all agencies in the Venice area. Prior to the formation of the joint venture, the hospital's referrals were spread among various DME agencies. These referral patterns changed after the creation of the venture. Post-venture, the hospital-affiliated company captured 85 percent of the referrals from Venice Hospital.

At issue in *Key Enterprises* was the hospital's change in policy regarding the role of home care coordinators in the DME referral process. Prior to the change, home care coordinators were responsible for assisting patients in selecting DME agencies. The home care coordinators at Venice Hospital were not hospital employees, but rather were employees of the various home care agencies that shared the home care coordinator role.[19] If the patient did not have a preference for a DME provider, the coordinator recommended one. The reality was that most patients did not have a choice of DME providers, and most patients requested a recommendation from the home care coordinator.

After formation of the joint venture, Venice directed the home care coordinators to adopt a default referral rule and refer all patients to the affiliated DME provider, absent specific patient or physician choice. The hospital prohibited outside DME representatives from meeting with the patients in the hospital. In contrast, the affiliated DME company's representatives were permitted to meet with patients in the hospital. Application of the default rule resulted in a dramatic increase in business for the affiliated DME company. Not surprisingly, referrals to the plaintiff decreased substantially, from 72 percent of the hospital's referrals prior to the affiliation to 30 percent after the affiliation.

The plaintiff brought suit under Sections 1 and 2 of the Sherman Antitrust Act alleging that the defendants engaged in numerous antitrust violations, including: (1) The hospital and its DME partner engaged in a reciprocal agreement with home care nurses whereby the nurses preferentially recommended the hospital-affiliated service; (2) the hospital changed its policy to

---

[18]   919 F.2d 1550 (11th Cir. 1990), *vacated* 979 F.2d 806 (11th Cir. 1992).

[19]   *Id.* at 1552 n.1.

deny DME vendors access to patients without any efficiency justification for the change; (3) employees of hospital-affiliated providers were allowed to hold themselves out as authorities who spoke on behalf of the hospital; (4) the DME venture partner (Sammett) entered into the venture to stifle competition; (5) the hospital maintained different standing orders for home health and DME; (6) the hospital applied a different default rule with regard to DME services that steered patients to the hospital-affiliated provider; and (7) the hospital leveraged its monopoly power in the acute care hospital market to avoid competition in the DME market.

Although the plaintiff won at trial, the trial court granted the defendants' motion for judgment notwithstanding the verdict, holding that there was insufficient evidence to support the plaintiff's claims. The Eleventh Circuit, however, reversed and reinstated the verdict, noting prominently the change in policy by the hospital that had previously granted equal access to patients and had not steered patients to DME vendors. The case eventually settled, but it became a model for these types of claims.

Many of the antitrust cases brought by downstream providers such as home health agencies are predicated on the assumption that a hospital has a duty to cooperate with such downstream providers allowing them access to hospital patients or referring patients directly to the providers. The plaintiffs in these cases often allege that the defendant hospital engaged in an improper refusal to deal.

The initial assumption in refusal to deal cases is that a firm, even one with market power, is under no obligation to cooperate with its rivals.[20] Nevertheless, this principle is not absolute, as there may be limited circumstances where a firm may not terminate an existing cooperative agreement. This was the case in *Aspen Skiing Co. v. Aspen Highlands Skiing Corp.*[21]

In *Aspen Skiing*, the United States Supreme Court held that a ski lodge acted anticompetitively when it terminated its participation in a joint, four-ski resort ticket program. Under the joint ticket program, skiers could purchase one joint ticket that would allow them to utilize the slopes at both Aspen Skiing and its rival, Aspen Highlands Skiing. By all accounts, the joint ticket program was beneficial to both resorts and was desired by tourists. Aspen Skiing, the defendant, was the larger of the two rivals and controlled three of the four ski slopes in question. After Aspen Skiing canceled its participation in the program, the plaintiff's share of the market declined. The only explanation offered by Aspen Skiing for its refusal to continue to participate in the joint ticket program was that the program could not be properly monitored. Highlands contended that the termination of the joint

[20] Monsanto Co. v. Spray-Rite Serv. Corp., 465 U.S. 752, 761 (1984).
[21] 472 U.S. 585 (1985).

ticket program constituted a prohibited refusal to deal under Section 2 of the Sherman Antitrust Act, and a jury agreed.

The Supreme Court agreed. Although the Court affirmed the general proposition that a firm has no duty to assist its competitors, the Court noted that the right to refuse to cooperate is not unqualified. In analyzing the issue, the Court ruled that it is critical to examine the effect of defendant's actions on consumers:

> The question whether Ski Co.'s conduct may properly be characterized as exclusionary cannot be answered by simply considering its effect on Highlands. In addition, it is relevant to consider its impact on consumers and whether it has impaired competition in an unnecessarily restrictive way. If a firm has been "attempting to exclude rivals on some basis other than efficiency," it is fair to characterize its behavior as predatory. It is, accordingly, appropriate to examine the effect of the challenged pattern of conduct on consumers, on Ski Co.'s smaller rival, and on Ski Co. itself.[22]

Finding no merit in the business justifications of the defendant, the court affirmed the jury verdict in favor of plaintiff.

The principle announced in *Aspen* may have been limited by the Supreme Court's later decision in *Verizon Communications, Inc. v. Trinko*.[23] That case involved a claim that Verizon's refusal to allow other telephone carriers access to their lines constituted an antitrust violation. Unlike in *Aspen*, however, there was no prior relationship between Verizon and the other carriers. Accordingly, the Supreme Court stated its intention to narrowly construe the *Aspen Skiing* holding, which, the Court noted, "is at or near the outer boundary of § 2 liability."[24] *Trinko,* accordingly, limited the applicability of *Aspen Skiing* to those cases in which competitors maintained preexisting cooperative agreements. Absent such preexisting relationships, there is no duty to cooperate. Additional cases have likewise limited *Aspen* to situations where there is a preexisting cooperation with the rival that is terminated without a valid precompetitive justification.[25]

An ancillary argument made by some downstream providers is that they are entitled to an equitable share of referrals from the acute care hospital and

---

[22] *Id.* at 605.

[23] 540 U.S. 398, 401 (2004).

[24] *Id.* at 409.

[25] *See* Transhorn, Ltd. v. United Techs. Corp. (In re Elevator Antitrust Litig.), 502 F.3d 47 (2d Cir.2007) dismissing class action by purchasers of elevators alleging that elevator companies refused to allow outside maintenance companies to service elevators).

that patients are "channeled" to a hospital-based home care organization. Indeed, utilization of a "default" referral policy has been the subject of cases brought by downstream healthcare entities. These policies acknowledge that few patients have a preference with regard to home care or post-hospitalization providers and, accordingly, seek recommendations from hospital discharge planners. In most cases, the hospital discharge planner recommends the hospital-based provider because that is the provider with whom he or she is most familiar. As to the core issue of whether mere "channeling" of patients to an affiliated downstream provider can constitute anticompetitive conduct, the Eastern District of Pennsylvania, in *Home Health Specialists*, rejected such a theory. There, the court held that such conduct, without some showing of increased price, reduction in supply, or decrease in quality, does not affect the competitive process as a whole:

> Encouraging, but not forcing, patients to choose one home health-care agency over another does not, in and of itself, make out an injury to competition. Because there is no showing of increased prices, reduction in supply, or decrease in quality, Plaintiff has not made out an injury to competition.[26]

A hospital's entry into the home health market on its own coupled with exclusion of other home health providers from access to hospital patients could give rise to claims of monopolization or attempted monopolization. This would depend on the relevant market and the parties' power within the market, among other factors. Similarly, should a home health agency that has a relationship with a particular DME supplier be denied access to the hospital's patients because the hospital wanted to develop its own DME business, monopoly issues could arise. This is especially so if, for instance, before the exclusionary policy was put into effect the hospital freely granted privileges to a number of home health agencies that dealt with a number of DME suppliers.[27]

Although threats from proprietary ancillary service providers who rely on hospitals for referrals remain a real risk, there are multiple steps that counsel can take to minimize the likelihood of such litigation. Often, these types of disputes can be risk-managed through appropriate policies to deal with downstream referrals and through proper education of hospital employees who are in a position to refer patients to such downstream providers. At the core

---

[26] Home Health Specialists, 1994 U.S. Dist. LEXIS 11947 at *15-16 (citations omitted).

[27] *E.g.*, Key Enterprises of Delaware, Inc. v. Venice Hospital, 919 F.2d 1550 (11th Cir. 1990), *vacated*, 979 F.2d 806 (11th Cir. 1992), *dismissed as moot*, 9 F.3rd 893 (11th Cir. 1993); M&M Medical Supplies and Service, Inc. v. Pleasant Valley Hospital, Inc., 981 F.2d 160 (4th Cir. 1992).

of many of these disputes is the notion that patients have the ultimate right to select the downstream provider. Indeed, 42 U.S.C. § 1395a requires that patient choice be honored.

Utilization of clear written policies and guidelines regarding the referral of patients to downstream providers is also critical. Such policies should affirmatively state that patient choice predominates over all other concerns. In many cases, however, the patient may not have a preference. In these cases, the policy should specify the steps that will be taken. Often, a scripted statement from the individual making such a referral will assist in ensuring that consistent information is provided to the patient. In all such situations, the issue must be discussed with the patient and/or family members so that they fully understand the process.

3.5 MAY A HOSPITAL REQUIRE THAT PHYSICIANS EMPLOYED BY THE SYSTEM REFER ALL CASES TO THE HOSPITAL?

Generally, yes, as long as the patient does not voice a preference for a different hospital or the referral is questionable from a patient safety standpoint. Moreover, as hospital employees, the physicians would presumably be incapable of conspiring with their employer, obviating any Section 1 concerns.[28] An issue may arise if, for example, such referrals would foreclose a substantial part of the market and thereby create an exclusionary practice that adversely affects competition. Even if this were the case, however, if the hospital provided substantial procompetitive justifications for the practice, it might very well pass muster under the rule of reason.

The issue is whether the referral creates an illegal tie or an improper refusal to deal. An illegal tie occurs when a seller exploits its control over the tying product to force the buyer into the purchase of a tied product that the buyer did not want at all or might have preferred to purchase elsewhere on different terms.[29] Here, the argument would be that the hospital is forcing patients to purchase hospital and related services as a condition of purchasing physician services. This argument presupposes that the patient is actually forced to purchase such services. To prevent a claim of forcing, patient choice should be honored; therefore, the key issue is whether the policy "forces" the buyer to purchase services from hospital. If the patient does not have a preference and if such choice by a payer or patient is honored, then a strong

---

[28] *See, e.g.,* Okusami v. Psychiatric Institute of Washington, 959 F.2d 1062, 1065 (D.C. Cir. 1992).

[29] Jefferson Parrish Hosp. Dist. No. 2 v. Hyde, 466 U.S. 2 (1984).

argument can be made that there is no forcing, and accordingly, no tying. Mere indifference by the patient should not be construed as forcing the patient to purchase such services.

> Tying arrangements need only be condemned if they restrain competition on the merits by forcing purchases that would not otherwise be made. A lack of price or quality competition does not create this type of forcing. If consumers lack price conscious-ness, that fact will not force them to take an anesthesiologist whose services they do not want—their indifference to price will have no impact on their willingness or ability to go to another hospital where they can utilize the services of the anesthesiolo-gist of their choice. Similarly, if consumers cannot evaluate the quality of [medical] services, it follows that they are indifferent between [providers of medical services] even in the absence of a tying arrangement—such an arrangement cannot be said to have foreclosed a choice that would have otherwise been made "on the merits."[30]

A central issue is whether there are anticompetitive effects from the practice. This inquiry, as with most in antitrust law, requires an analysis of the potential for the exercise of market power and whether the practice will foreclose substantial competition. In the example above, if the physicians (the tying product) have substantial market power, then the practice could give rise to a colorable claim. If, for example, the hospital employed substan-tially all of the primary care physicians in the area, then the requirement that they refer all general surgery patients to a hospital-employed surgeon might require further scrutiny. Conversely, if the hospital's primary care physicians did not constitute a majority of the primary care physicians in the area, then there is less likelihood that the practice would be deemed anticompetitive.

Second, the practice may be analyzed as an exclusive dealing arrangement. Here the focus will again be on whether the practice substantially forecloses competition. As addressed by the Supreme Court:

> In determining whether an exclusive-dealing contract is unrea-sonable, the proper focus is on the structure of the market for the products or services in question—the number of sellers and buyers in the market, the volume of their business, and the ease with which buyers and sellers can redirect their purchases or sales to others. Exclusive dealing is an unreasonable restraint on trade

---

[30] *Id.* at 28.

only when a significant fraction of buyers or sellers are frozen out of a market by the exclusive deal.[31]

Thus, as with the tying analysis, the issue is whether the hospital and the physicians have substantial market power to affect the competitive process. For example, if the physicians are necessary referral sources and the practice would foreclose a substantial part of the market, then the policy may require further analysis. Alternatively, if there are significant alternative referral sources available to the physicians, then the requirement that employed physicians refer only to hospital-affiliated providers would not likely result in any anticompetitive harm.

A related concept is whether the policy is a form of economic credentialing. By itself, economic credentialing usually does not run afoul of the antitrust laws because, typically, little competition is actually foreclosed. It is, however, easy to formulate a scenario where economic credentialing is part of a pattern of anticompetitive activity undertaken by a hospital with market power that could harm competition.

Moreover, the practice of economic credentialing is increasingly being scrutinized under state law. For example, the Arkansas Supreme Court has unanimously rejected a hospital system's economic credentialing policy, ruling that the facility was unjustified in denying staff privileges to a group of physicians with an ownership stake in a competing specialty hospital.[32] The court upheld a 2009 trial court decision that found Baptist Health's policy of restricting privileges based on financial concerns interfered with patient-physician relationships and suppressed competition, in violation of state laws.

There, Little Rock-based Baptist, the largest hospital system in Arkansas, instituted its economic conflict-of-interest policy in 2003, causing twelve staff cardiologists who owned a competing specialty heart hospital to lose their privileges. The physicians sued. The high court's final ruling permanently bars Baptist from enforcing its policy. The court found that:

> Baptist's motive was to discourage competition by physicians who considered investing in specialty hospitals, and Baptist wanted to force patients to choose between it and [their doctors], [and] [t]he [plaintiffs'] interest was in patient-physician relationships and continuity of care, which outweighed Baptist's interest

---

[31] *Id.* at 45.

[32] Baptist Health v. Murphy, 2010 Ark. 358 (Sept. 30, 2010). The court did, however, reverse a portion of the lower court ruling that Baptist's policy violated the state's Deceptive Trade Practices Act.

in protecting its economic viability because no evidence supports Baptist's purported need for the policy.[33]

Economic credentialing can be a way to try and steer referrals from non-employee physicians away from certain competing hospitals. Nevertheless, such policies are replete with both political and legal issues and are assured of being challenged by excluded practitioners; therefore, caution is necessary before implementing such policies.[34]

---

[33]   *Baptist Health,* 2010 Ark. 358 at 25.

[34]   Economic credentialing is addressed more thoroughly in Chapter 2.

4

Physician and Other Healthcare Provider Networks[1]

David M. Narrow, Esquire

4.1 WHAT ANTITRUST CONCERNS ARISE REGARDING PHYSICIAN OR OTHER HEALTHCARE PROVIDER NETWORKS?

The primary antitrust concern that arises in physician and other healthcare provider networks is the elimination of competition among participants providing the same types of services in the network—termed a *horizontal restraint of trade*. Typically, this loss of competition involves agreements on the prices that the providers will charge for their services to payers, such as insurers, Blues plans, health maintenance organizations (HMOs), and other payer organizations. In addition to agreements on price, these arrangements often include other

---

[1] The discussion here will be limited to network arrangements involving physicians. The same or similar legal principles apply regarding networks that involve other categories of competing healthcare providers—dentists, podiatrists, psychologists, nurse practitioners, pharmacists, hospitals, ambulance services, etc. However, the factual circumstances, including their capabilities and available mechanisms for jointly achieving efficiencies, may vary across disciplines. Additionally, networks that involve more than one discipline, e.g., physician-hospital organizations (PHOs), potentially raise vertical antitrust issues that are beyond the scope of this chapter. However, these will rarely, if ever, raise issues that could result in *per se* condemnation or criminal liability. The Department of Justice and the Federal Trade Commission have issued enforcement policy statements on how they will analyze provider networks under the antitrust laws. (*See Statements of Antitrust Enforcement Policy in Health Care* (August 1996), 4 Trade Reg. Rep. (CCH) Par. 13,153), *available at* http://www.ftc. gov/bc/healthcare/industryguide/policy/index/htm. Physician network joint ventures are discussed in Statement 8, and multi-provider networks (those involving various categories of nonphysician healthcare providers, or involving more than one category of provider) are addressed in Statement 9.

terms of dealing related to payment terms and numerous other factors that may affect costs and prices.

Although the healthcare providers in a network undertake some joint activity through the network, they nevertheless remain competitors of one another for services offered outside the arrangement, and to some extent, compete for patients within the network.[2] Thus, network providers may partially integrate with one another through participation in the network but generally will not totally merge their entire medical practices through such arrangements.

Network arrangements typically involve jointly selling (i.e., contracting to sell) to payers or purchasers of the providers' services at terms (including price) that are jointly agreed on by the competing providers in the network. Thus, many insurance companies, Blues plans, HMOs, or administrative arrangements may contract with organizations of providers to actually provide the medical and other healthcare services that the payers offer to their enrollees.[3] The antitrust concern in such networks is that independently practicing physicians are agreeing on the terms, including prices, at which they will offer and provide their services in the marketplace. This, on its face, eliminates previously-existing or potential competition among those providers.[4] By combining in selling their services, the participants may create sufficient market power that their agreed-upon prices prevail in the market, or influence the level

---

[2] Physicians in an independent physician association (IPA), for example, still will compete with each other regarding patients whose medical services are not provided through payer arrangements with the IPA. Physicians in a network—at least if they are paid on a fee-for-service basis—also still will compete with one another to treat individual patients who are served by the network. Thus, a patient who is treated by Dr. A under a program where services are provided by the network will necessarily not be treated by Drs. B, C, and D for those same services, even though all the doctors are in the same network. This type of arrangement contrasts with a partnership or a merger, where all the monies earned by any participant typically are credited to the partnership or merged entity, regardless of which individual provider "earned" the fee by providing the specific services.

[3] Payers may contract with established provider networks, or may create their own networks by contracting individually with physicians or group practices.

[4] It is important to understand that *price*, as the antitrust laws define it, can involve any aspect of payment that affects the price, such as price discounts, credit terms, or requirements as to when or how quickly payment will be made. *See, e.g.*, Catalano, Inc. v. Target Sales, Inc., 446 U.S. 643 (1980). Similarly, even an agreement by sellers on a starting price from which ultimate sale prices to buyers will be negotiated individually between the buyer and seller has been held to be an illegal price agreement. Plymouth Dealers' Ass'n. of N. Cal. v. U.S., 279 Fed 2d 128 (9th Cir. 1960).

of market prices, rather than having prices derived from market competition among those physicians.[5]

Absent appropriate justifying circumstances, antitrust law views agreement on prices by competitors (and its flip side, jointly agreeing not to sell their services, except on jointly agreed-upon price terms) as perhaps the most clearly anticompetitive and prohibited conduct. Such conduct is considered *per se* illegal, i.e., presumptively illegal without the need to show actual harm to competition or the existence of market power, and not subject to justifying defenses, such as that the prices are "reasonable."[6] Joining together by competitors solely to increase market power (clout) and collectively obtain higher prices is behavior typical of cartels, has frequently been challenged by the antitrust enforcement agencies, and even may be subject to criminal prosecution.

The antitrust laws are also concerned about certain other activities that may occur when competitors get together, such as boycotts of competitors, market division or customer allocation schemes, tying arrangements, monopolization, and mergers and acquisitions that aggregate and create market power among the participants. However, these types of activities have occurred much less frequently in the context of healthcare provider networks than agreements regarding price and other terms of dealing among network participants, and joint negotiation of those terms with purchasers and payers.

Most importantly, to avoid stifling innovation and legitimate, productive ventures, the courts and the antitrust enforcement agencies have applied the antitrust laws in ways that attempt to distinguish between plainly anticompetitive arrangements that raise prices and hurt consumers, and other joint conduct among competitors that, even though it may restrict some participant competition, appears intended and likely to enhance overall efficiency and create, rather than eliminate, competition in the market—all to the benefit of consumers. Thus, the Supreme Court long ago determined that only "unreasonable" restraints of trade are prohibited by the antitrust laws,[7] and the courts developed analytical approaches to distinguish "naked" price agreements and other restraints of trade from ones that were necessary to facilitate ultimately procompetitive cooperative joint ventures among otherwise independent competitors.

---

[5] *See, e.g.,* Arizona v. Maricopa County Medical Society, 457 U.S. 332, 356 (1982). "Their [the physicians'] combination [in the form of network-like foundations for medical care] has merely permitted them to sell their services to certain customers at fixed prices and arguably to affect the prevailing market price of medical care."

[6] *Catalano at, Inc.* 647; United States v. Socony-Vacuum Oil Co., Inc., 310 U.S. 150, 210, 218 (1940); United States v. Trenton Potteries Co., 273 U.S. 392, 396, 397, 398-99 (1927); United States v. Trans-Missouri Freight Ass'n., 166 U.S. 290, 340-341 (1897).

[7] Standard Oil Co. v. United States, 221 U.S. 1 (1911); American Tobacco Co. v. United States 221 U.S. 106 (1911); State Oil v. Kahn, 522 U.S. 3, 10 (1997).

4.2 WHAT TYPES OF PROVIDER NETWORK ARRANGEMENTS ARE PERMISSIBLE UNDER THE ANTITRUST LAWS?

There are a variety of types of healthcare provider network arrangements that either will not raise antitrust concerns at all, or that will avoid *per se* condemnation because they appear likely to enhance overall efficiency, increase competition, and benefit consumers.

First, if an arrangement does not involve an agreement in restraint of trade—either because there is no agreement, or because any agreement in fact does not restrain trade—the conduct involved cannot be unlawful.[8] In the healthcare area, various networks exist whose participants are not actual or potential competitors. Typically, however, these networks involve ambulance services or other geographically dispersed healthcare providers who join together to offer a service that no single participant alone could provide.[9] From an antitrust standpoint, these networks do not eliminate competition because the participants are not competitors. By coming together to offer something that the individual participants, acting alone, could not, the arrangements effectively create new competitors in the market, offering alternatives that previously did not exist. In that regard, such ventures are viewed as affirmatively procompetitive arrangements.

---

[8] Whether or not competitors or others have agreed with one another is always a factual determination. Agreement, however, can be demonstrated directly, or inferred by indirect, circumstantial evidence. Even if there is an agreement, however, to be unlawful it must affect competition regarding some commercial activity. For example, one court has held that an agreement by a professional association to label a particular medical procedure "experimental," without adopting any further actions in that regard, did not violate the antitrust laws. The court stated that "[t]here can be no restraint of trade without a restraint," concluding that the labeling of the procedure was not such a competitive restraint. Schachar v. American Academy of Ophthalmology, 870 F.2d 397 (7th Cir. 1989).

[9] *See, e.g.,* Letter from Robert F. Leibenluft, Assistant Director, Health Care Services and Products Division, Bureau of Competition, Federal Trade Commission to Timothy C. Cashmore (Dec. 22, 1997) (Alliance of Independent Medical Services, L.L.C.) (*available at* http://www.ftc.gov/bc/adops/aims.fin.shtm). Letter from Robert F. Leibenluft, Assistant Director, Health Care Services and Products Division, Bureau of Competition, Federal Trade Commission to John A. Cook, Esq. (Jan. 30, 1997) (Mobile Health Resources, L.L.C.) (*available at* http://www.ftc.gov/bc/adops/mobil.shtm). *See also* Letter from Mark J. Horoschak, Assistant Director, Bureau of Competition, Federal Trade Commission to J. Bert Morgan (Nov. 17, 1993) (California Managed Imaging Medical Group, Inc.) (*available at* http://www.ftc.gov/bc/adops/011.shtm).

A second type of network arrangement that potentially can avoid antitrust concerns, while still involving actual or potential competitors, is what has been called a *messenger model* network.

Messenger models may take a variety of forms of operation, and properly are intended to facilitate agreements between individual network providers and payers. Messenger models may reduce the administrative and transaction costs of the parties reaching agreements. The key common element to a lawful messenger model is that it operates in a way that avoids any agreement on prices and other competitively sensitive terms of dealing among the individual network members and does not facilitate any agreement or coordination regarding acceptance or rejection of offers from payers. This type of arrangement is discussed in several Federal Trade Commission (FTC) advisory opinions and Department of Justice business review letters.[10]

The greatest concern regarding messenger model arrangements is that they may not operate in practice to ensure the network providers make independent, individual decisions regarding payer offers to participate in a program. Rather, messenger models, in practice, may involve a variety of activities—from jointly negotiating with payers the terms to be offered to network providers, rejecting payer offers and refusing to forward them to individual network members, coordinating or encouraging particular provider responses, or engaging in various other activities that facilitate coordination—that render the messenger arrangement ineffective and unlawful.[11] The FTC has brought several cases against provider networks for price fixing and collective negotiations with payers against such networks.

The third approach for a provider network to avoid condemnation as a *per se* illegal price-fixing arrangement is to demonstrate that the network is a legitimate joint venture involving substantial integration among the competing participants that has the potential to generate consumer-benefiting efficiencies. Such *integrated joint ventures* are analyzed under the ancillary restraints

---

[10] *See, e.g.,* Letter from Jeffrey W. Brennan, Assistant Director, Health Care Services and Products Division, Bureau of Competition, Federal Trade Commission to Martin J. Thompson (Sept. 23, 2003) (Bay Area Preferred Physicians) (*available at* http://www.ftc.gov/bc/adops/bapp030923.shtm).

[11] *See* Jeff Miles, "Ticking Antitrust Bombs: A Message to Messed up Messenger Models," 6 *Health Lawyers News* 4 (American Health Lawyers Association, November 2002), which identifies many ways in which messenger model arrangements deviate from behavior that such arrangements must engage in, if they are to operate lawfully. An additional difficulty with using a messenger model arrangement is that, if it is properly implemented, its primary efficiency is limited to reducing the transaction costs to network providers of having to individually evaluate multiple payer offers. This may be viewed by some as an inadequate justification for implementing what can be a fairly cumbersome mechanism for dealing with payer offers.

doctrine to ascertain whether the restraints are reasonably necessary to the joint venture's achieving the potential efficiencies.[12] If justified, they then will be evaluated more fully under the antitrust Rule of Reason that assesses the arrangement's market power and balances the joint venture's procompetitive and anticompetitive effects in assessing its legality.

4.3   WHAT MUST A PROVIDER NETWORK THAT INVOLVES AGREEMENT AMONG COMPETITORS DO TO DEMONSTRATE THAT IT IS INTEGRATED, MAY QUALIFY FOR RULE-OF-REASON TREATMENT, AND ULTIMATELY MAY BE LAWFUL?

First, to be considered an integrated joint venture, the network must involve some interconnectedness among its participants that evidences that it is more than the mere assembly of independent competing providers for the purposes of agreeing on prices and selling their services on jointly determined terms, or aggregating market power. Integration joins the participants in some common productive, efficiency-enhancing, and potentially procompetitive endeavor that operates to motivate the participants to be concerned about the joint venture's business success or failure, rather than just their own personal economic welfare as individual competitors.

4.4   WHAT IS MEANT BY *EFFICIENCY*?

Typically, such things as lower costs and improved quality are considered efficiencies. If a provider network can demonstrate other types of efficiencies that result from its formation and operation, these certainly will be considered. Integrating administrative and contracting functions through a network may create some efficiencies for network participants and its payer customers (e.g., reduced costs from having a preassembled network, and avoiding the time, effort, and expense associated with each provider having to individually assess and respond to each payer contract offer, etc.). Although these types of transaction cost efficiencies may be real, they are unlikely to be of sufficient magnitude alone to justify the loss of price competition from joint contracting by network providers regarding their underlying professional services.

---

[12]   The analytical approach regarding ancillary restraints was first articulated and applied by Judge (later Justice) Taft in United States v. Addyston Pipe & Steel Co., 85 F. 271 (6th Cir. 1898).

Indeed, every naked price fixing cartel offers a certain level of efficiencies of this type.[13]

Achieving cost and quality efficiencies in providing healthcare services frequently involves adoption and implementation of uniform best practices standards; electronic or other systems to collect performance data (such as rates of utilization of expensive services and associated costs), providing both individual and collective performance evaluation information to providers; a system for provider education and remediation of substandard performance; and a myriad of other possible systems and mechanisms to improve the providers' individual and collective performance.

4.5 WHAT ARE ACCEPTABLE WAYS FOR PROVIDERS TO INTEGRATE THROUGH A NETWORK TO QUALIFY FOR RULE-OF-REASON ANALYSIS?

The antitrust laws do not dictate how healthcare providers (or any other joint ventures among competitors) must integrate through a network or other joint venture. However, case law and guidance from the antitrust enforcement agencies identify several ways that are likely to demonstrate integration by competitors, and potentially prevent the arrangement from being summarily condemned as anticompetitive and illegal. Perhaps more important, various examples of certain forms of integration have arisen in healthcare markets as healthcare providers' groups have attempted to jointly work to improve quality and lower the costs of providing medical and other healthcare services.

Financial integration is one way that competitors can come together in a joint venture. Financial integration, as discussed by the Supreme Court in *Maricopa*, is one way to avoid *per se* condemnation. There, the Court held that certain medical care foundations—networks of physicians that agreed to offer their members' medical care services to payers at agreed-upon maximum prices—were engaged in *per se* illegal price fixing. The Court held that the foundations did not allow the physicians in them to do anything other than sell their individual services at agreed prices, and contrasted the foundations to other types of arrangements that were "analogous to partner-

---

[13] However, in Nat'l. Collegiate Athletic Ass'n. v. Bd. of Regents of the Univ. of Oklahoma, 468 U.S. 85 (1984), the Supreme Court characterized as follows its earlier decision in Broadcast Music, Inc. v. CBS, Inc., 441 U.S. 1 (1979) (holding that an arrangement among competing sellers of individual music licenses to offer a blanket license to use copyrighted musical compositions at an agreed-upon fee was subject to rule-of-reason analysis, rather than per se condemnation): *"Broadcast Music* squarely holds that a joint selling arrangement may be so efficient that it will increase sellers' aggregate output and thus be procompetitive." 468 U.S. at 103.

ships or other joint arrangements in which persons who would otherwise be competitors pool their capital and share the risks of loss as well as the opportunities for profit. In such joint ventures, the partnership is regarded as a single firm competing with other sellers in the market."[14] The Court went on to say that "[i]f a clinic offered complete medical coverage for a flat fee, the cooperating doctors would have the type of partnership arrangement in which a price-fixing agreement among the doctors would be perfectly proper."[15]

Experience has shown that there are a variety of ways in healthcare provider networks that the participants can pool their finances and share the risks of profit or loss from their collective performance. This sometimes takes the form of the network participants sharing substantial financial risk—either or both downside and upside—regarding the success or failure of the entire network in providing cost-effective, covered services to contracted payers' enrollees. If the network providers together are effective in controlling the costs of treating enrollees through more appropriate use of expensive services, they may share in the payer's savings. If the network providers fail to do so, they may incur financial penalties.

Among the ways for providers in network joint ventures to financially integrate are accepting capitated payments for all necessary treatment of patients for a specified period, use of global payments or bundled fees for an extended treatment (e.g., maternity services), use of percentage of premium arrangements with payers (allocating a fixed amount for certain treatment areas), or using certain payment-withhold pools to apply penalties for excessive expenses or rewards for more efficient use of services. The *Health Care Statements* identify a variety of these forms and also recognize that other such financial integration forms may arise through sharing risk and reward in the industry.[16] The *Health Care Statements* also provide antitrust "safety zones"

---

[14] 457 U.S. at 356.

[15] *Id.* at 357.

[16] Regarding programs that appear to involve the sharing of substantial financial risk, substance will prevail over form in assessing whether an arrangement involves such risk sharing. For example, two proposed programs, each involving a 15 percent withhold from the payments to physicians in the programs received different conclusions from the FTC in this regard, based on the overall facts involved. *See* Letter from Mark J. Horoschak, Assistant Director, Bureau of Competition, Federal Trade Commission to Paul W. McVay (July 5, 1994) (*available at* http://www.ftc.gov/bc/adops/007.shtm) and Letter from from Mark J. Horoschak to George Q. Evans (July 5, 1994) (*available at* http://www.ftc.gov/bc/adops/006.shtm).

for certain financially integrated physician networks that clearly lack market power and thus pose little, if any, risk to competition.[17]

Alternatively, providers may clinically integrate. Although this form of integration has not specifically been addressed by the courts, the efficiency-enhancing potential of such arrangements is accepted by healthcare industry experts[18] and it is recognized by the federal antitrust enforcement agencies in the *Health Care Statements* as a potential form of efficiency-enhancing integration. In essence, *clinical integration* involves a network adopting particular systems and mechanisms to control costs and improve quality in the provision of network providers' healthcare services, even in the absence of financial risk-sharing as an incentive to motivate such desired behavior.[19]

The FTC evaluated the potential legal issues regarding a number of specific proposed clinically integrated healthcare provider networks, and issued staff advisory opinions regarding them.[20] Following the analysis described in

---

[17]   No safety zones are provided for nonphysician, or multiprovider networks because the agencies lacked sufficient experience with these arrangements to reliably predict their competitive effects in advance.

[18]   Knowledgeable commentators have emphasized the importance of systematized approaches—sometimes referred to as "organized processes"—in achieving the potential efficiency benefits of clinical integration arrangements among otherwise independently practicing physicians. *See, e.g.,* L. P. Casalino, *The Federal Trade Commission, Clinical Integration, and the Organization of Physician Practice,* 31 J. of Health Politics, Policy and Law 569 at 580-81 (June 2006) ("[T]here is ample evidence both that the use by physician groups of organized processes to improve quality is effective and that it is uncommon [citations omitted]. The processes suggested by the FTC clinical integration policy are consistent with the literature on quality improvement . . . ."); L. P. Casalino, R. R. Gillies, et al., "External Incentives, Information Technology, and Organized Processes to Improve Health Care Quality for Patients with Chronic Diseases," 289 *JAMA* 434 (January 22/29, 2003); and S. M. Shortell and L. P. Casalino, "Health Care Reform Requires Accountable Care Systems," 300 *JAMA* 95 (July 2, 2008) (An accountable care system is ". . . an entity that can implement organized processes for improving the quality and controlling the costs of care and be held accountable for the results.").

[19]   Some networks may supplement their efforts at clinical integration by also including financial risks or rewards —forms of financial integration. There also may be other ways to integrate and improve efficiency through network arrangements in healthcare besides financial and clinical integration, and the antitrust enforcement agencies state in the *Health Care Statements* that they will consider these, as well, should they arise. This is consistent with antitrust joint venture law generally, which does not specify or limit the ways that competitors can join together to increase efficiency through a joint venture.

[20]   *See, e.g.,* Letter from Jeffrey W. Brennan, Assistant Director, Bureau of Competition, Federal Trade Commission, to John J. Miles (February 19, 2002) (MedSouth, Inc.) (*available at* http://www.ftc.gov/bc/adops/medsouth.htm); letter from David R. Pender, Acting Assistant Directr, Bureau of Competition, to Clifton

the *Health Care Statements*, these advisory opinions first assess whether the networks involve substantial integration by the network participants that is likely to lead to the achievement of significant efficiencies in their provision of services.

However, as discussed below, this is only the first step in the analysis.

4.6 IF WE ARE INTEGRATED, CAN WE AGREE ON PRICES AND OTHER TERMS UNDER CONTRACT TO SELL OUR SERVICES TO PAYERS OR OTHER PURCHASERS?

Possibly, but not necessarily. Once the venture's potentially beneficial integration is demonstrated, the analysis then looks at the nature, extent, purposes, and justifications for the specific competitive restraints that are occurring as part of the joint venture's formation and operation. The competitive restraints at issue must be "ancillary," i.e., subordinate to the joint venture's legitimate and procompetitive purposes and activities, and reasonably necessary to the venture's achievement of those efficiencies.[21] Therefore, if the joint venture's

---

E. Johnson (March 28, 2006) (Suburban Health Organization), *available at* http://www. ftc.gov/os/2006/03/SuburbanHealthOrganizationStaffAdvisoryOpinion 03282006. pdf); Letter from Markus H. Meier, Assistant Director, Bureau of Competition, Federal Trade Commission to John J. Miles (June 18, 2007)(MedSouth, Inc. follow-up letter) (*available at* http://www.ftc.gov/bc/adops/070618medsouth.pdf); Letter from Markus H. Meier, Assistant Director, Bureau of Competition, Federal Trade Commission, to Christi J. Braun and John J. Miles (September 17, 2007) (Greater Rochester Independent Practice Association, Inc.) (*available at* http://www.ftc.gov/bc/adops/gripa.pdf); Letter from Markus H. Meier, Assistant Director, Bureau of Competition, Federal Trade Commission, to Christi J. Braun (April 13, 2009) (TriState Health Partners, Inc.) (*available at* http://www.ftc.gov/os/closings/staff/090413tristateaoletter.pdf).

[21] Judge Bork provides an extended description of how the ancillary restraints analysis is applied in Rothery Storage & Van Co. v. Atlas Van Lines, 792 F.2d 210 (D.C. Cir. 1986), *cert. denied* 479 U.S. 1033 (1987). ("To be ancillary, and hence exempt from the per se rule, an agreement eliminating competition must be subordinate and collateral to a separate, legitimate transaction. The ancillary restraint is subordinate and collateral in the sense that it serves to make the main transaction more effective in accomplishing its purpose. . . . [T]he restraint imposed must be related to the efficiency sought to be achieved. If it is so broad that part of the restraint suppresses competition without creating efficiency, the restraint is, to that extent, not ancillary."). 792 F.2d at 224. One court has opined that there needs to be an "organic connection between the restraint and the cooperative needs of the enterprise that would allow . . . [the court] to call the restraint a merely ancillary one." General Leaseways, Inc. v. Nat'l. Truck Leasing Ass'n., 744 F.2d 588, 595 (7th cir. 1984). The Federal Trade Commission has applied a variant of the ancillary restraints analysis in its decisions in *Polygram Holding, Inc.* and *North Texas Specialty Physicians*. In *NTSP*, the Commission stated

efficiencies can reasonably be achieved without the competitive restraints, or with significantly less elimination of competition, the loss of competition from the restraints is not considered reasonably justified.[22] Nevertheless, antitrust analysis does contemplate that some elimination of competition among a joint venture's participants may be reasonable and may be necessary to its successful operation in the market, or even its very existence.

(at p. 13, n.20) that "[t]he concept of ancillary restraints . . . is subsumed in the Commission's *Polygram* analysis," and quoted from that opinion to the effect that "[t]he ancillary restraints doctrine retains its vitality in evaluating efficiency claims." It also noted that the Commission's "use [of] the terminology of *Polygram* rather than the terminology of ancillary restraints . . . does not mean that we disagree with . . . [that] alternative analysis." *See also* Federal Trade Commission and U.S. Department of Justice, *Antitrust Guidelines for Collaborations Among Competitors* (April 2000) (*available at* http://www.ftc.gov/os/2000/04/ftcdojguidelines.pdf).

[22] Antitrust law does not require that any restraint be the absolutely least competitively restrictive alternative possible, but only that the restraint be one that is reasonably necessary to achieving the integrated venture's efficiencies. *See* Federal Trade Commission and Department of Justice, *Antitrust Guidelines for Collaborations Among Competitors* (April 2000) at Sect. 3.36(b) (*available at* http://www.ftc.gov/os/2000/04/ftcdojguidelines.pdf).

> The Agencies consider only those efficiencies for which the relevant agreement is reasonably necessary. An agreement may be "reasonably necessary" without being essential. However, if the participants could have achieved or could achieve similar efficiencies by practical, significantly less restrictive means, then the Agencies conclude that the relevant agreement is not reasonably necessary to their achievement. In making this assessment, the Agencies consider only alternatives that are practical in the business situation faced by the participants; the Agencies do not search for a theoretically less restrictive alternative that is not realistic given business realities.

> The reasonable necessity of an agreement may depend upon the market context and upon the duration of the agreement. An agreement that may be justified by the needs of a new entrant, for example, may not be reasonably necessary to achieve cognizable efficiencies in different market circumstances. The reasonable necessity of an agreement also may depend on whether it deters individual participants from undertaking free riding or other opportunistic conduct that could reduce significantly the ability of the collaboration to achieve cognizable efficiencies. Collaborations sometimes include agreements to discourage any one participant from appropriating an undue share of the fruits of the collaboration or to align participants' incentives to encourage cooperation in achieving the efficiency goals of the collaboration. The Agencies assess whether such agreements are reasonably necessary to deter opportunistic conduct that otherwise would likely prevent the achievement of cognizable efficiencies.

The network must also demonstrate that the participants' agreement on prices and other terms of dealing, joint contracting with payers, and any other competitive restraints effected through the network are subordinate to its legitimate and procompetitive purposes and activities and are reasonably necessary for the network to achieve the efficiencies and procompetitive effects that the network makes possible. Effectively doing so will result in the arrangement and its competitive restraints being evaluated under the antitrust Rule of Reason, rather than being summarily condemned as a *per se* illegal price fixing arrangement. However, if the joint venture includes restraints that are collateral—e.g., unrelated to the joint venture's legitimate purposes and activities, or not reasonably necessary to achieve the network's integrative efficiencies, it will be summarily condemned. An example would be the providers in a network agreeing on the prices they will charge to patients they treat outside the network.[23]

To be lawful, however, even an integrated network whose competitive restraints are ancillary nevertheless must not have market power—an assessment made only after the preceding aspects of the analysis have been completed. If it has market power—for example, if it includes such a large percentage of local physicians, and payers effectively must purchase services through the joint venture, even if integrated and involving only ancillary restraints, it still may be unlawful if it has market power, and thus can charge supracompetitive prices without the market being able to discipline such conduct.[24] This analysis occurs under the Rule-of-Reason analysis of the arrangement.

---

[23] *See, e.g.,* National Collegiate Athletic Ass'n. v. Bd. of Regents of the Univ. Of Oklahoma, 468 U.S. 85 (1984), where the Supreme Court agreed that league sports were a form of joint venture for which certain restrictions among the participants were essential to operate as a league. But the Court held that adoption of restrictions on the ability of members of the league to individually enter into arrangements for live television broadcasts of their teams' games was not necessary for the "product" of league sports, and was a restriction on output that was illegal. In essence, the Court held that the NCAA was a legitimate joint venture, but the restraint that it had adopted was not ancillary to achieving its legitimate purposes.

[24] To reduce or eliminate market power concerns, some healthcare provider networks operate on a nonexclusive basis regarding their provider participants. In such nonexclusive networks, the participants are free to join other networks or contract directly with payers that do not wish to contract through the network. This is intended to help ensure that such payers, if they wish, have access to adequate sources of healthcare providers in the market, at market prices, without having to deal with the network.

4.7 TO WHAT KINDS OF PROVIDER NETWORK ARRANGEMENTS DOES THIS ANALYSIS APPLY?

The type of joint venture analysis described above applies to virtually all arrangements that are made up of competing healthcare providers and that involve the partial integration of their activities. As noted previously, this involves some degree of integration by the participants, but not complete elimination of them as competitors of one another, as would be the case with a merger, such as in the formation of a group practice. For example, physicians in a network may have integrated regarding various aspects of the provision of care, cost containment activities, quality assurance activities, or centralized administrative tasks regarding patients for which the joint venture agrees to provide services. However, the participating providers still remain competitors of each other for individual patients who are not covered by programs for which the joint venture has agreed to provide services.[25]

The name or type of organization largely is irrelevant to how it will be analyzed under the antitrust laws. What matters is the arrangement's composition (whether it includes competing providers), and what those competing providers do (or do not do) through the arrangement, both to improve efficiency and to eliminate competition among the participants. Partially integrated arrangements may include individual physician associations (IPAs), physician-hospital organizations (PHOs), clinics without walls, and various other similar arrangements that involve the coming together of otherwise competing healthcare providers in networks. Accountable care organizations (ACOs) under the Medicare program also are a type of healthcare provider network joint venture, and receive similar, albeit somewhat different, treatment by the antitrust agencies (*see below*).

4.8 HOW CAN I GET GUIDANCE ABOUT WHETHER A PROVIDER NETWORK ARRANGEMENT IS PERMISSIBLE UNDER THE ANTITRUST LAWS?

Personal or corporate counsel generally can advise on these issues. Various professional and trade associations also have resources that may be helpful. In addition, for proposed (neither hypothetical nor already ongoing) conduct, the FTC, in proper situations, can issue advisory opinions under its Rules (*see* 16 C.F.R. Sects. 1.1 to 1.4). *Guidance from Staff of the*

---

[25] The formation of a totally merged entity typically would be analyzed under Section 7 of the Clayton Act, and possibly Section 2 of the Sherman Act (relating to monopolization).

Bureau of Competition's Health Care Division on Requesting and Obtaining an Advisory Opinion is available on the FTC's Web site at http://www.ftc.gov/bc/healthcare/industryguide/adv-opinionguidance.pdf. The Bureau of Competition's Health Care Division staff also is generally willing to provide less formal advice. The Department of Justice also issues business review letters, which are similar to advisory opinions. Information on requesting a business review letter can be found on the Department of Justice's Web site at http://www.justice.gov/atr/public/busreview/procedure.html.

4.9 WHAT ABOUT ACCOUNTABLE CARE ORGANIZATIONS THAT ARE ESTABLISHED AND OPERATE UNDER ARRANGEMENTS WITH CENTERS FOR MEDICARE & MEDICAID SERVICES UNDER THE MEDICARE PROGRAM AS PART OF THE HEALTH REFORM LAW?

ACOs are provider network arrangements pursuant to the Patient Protection and Affordable Care Act and the Health Care and Education Reconciliation Act of 2010 (collectively the Affordable Care Act) that have met requirements established by the Centers for Medicare & Medicaid Services (CMS) of the Department of Health and Human Services, and that have contracted to provide covered medical and other health services to beneficiaries pursuant to a contract entered into between the ACO and CMS. The ACO program seeks to improve quality and efficiency in the provision of these services, in part through the use of financial incentives (shared savings), and in some cases financial penalties as well, depending on the ACO's aggregate performance on a variety of quality and cost measures.

To the extent that these programs operate solely as part of the Medicare program, where CMS—i.e., the government—unilaterally sets the prices paid to the healthcare provider participants, the antitrust laws generally would not apply.[26] However, there has been much discussion about ACOs desiring to also offer their programs to private payers—commercial insurers, Blues

---

[26] Although the antitrust laws would not apply to the federal government deciding on the prices to be paid to ACO participants, the antitrust laws could apply to the ACOs if the competing providers either collectively agreed to refuse to deal with CMS at all, or attempted to force CMS to pay higher prices by refusing to deal, except at higher payment levels. *See, e.g.,* F.T.C. v. Superior Court Trial Lawyers Ass'n., 493 U.S. 427 (1990) holding that a boycott by trial lawyers of a government program to provide legal services to indigent defendants to obtain higher fees violated the antitrust laws; Michigan State Medical Society, 101 F.T.C. 191, 275-279, 296-301 (1983) in which a concerted refusal to deal with the Michigan Medicaid program by competing private physicians to obtain higher payments was held to violate the antitrust laws.

plans, self-insured employers, etc. If they were to do so, they would be subject to the same antitrust law standards as otherwise would apply to such network arrangements operating in the private sector.

Concern about this potential antitrust exposure for ACOs was identified as a possible disincentive for providers and provider groups to agree to participate in the ACO program. To avoid fears about possible antitrust liability undercutting development of the ACO program, the antitrust enforcement agencies adopted policies that provide somewhat more lenient treatment of the arrangements during the period when they are also under contract with CMS.[27] For example, the agencies have stated that, during the time an ACO is contracted with CMS and subject to its requirements and oversight, and because the ACO will be required to have a variety of systems and mechanisms to ensure the participants' integrated operation through the ACO, an ACO will be presumed by the agencies to involve substantial participant integration, and joint contracting with payers by the ACO will be presumptively considered ancillary to that integration. Hence, the ACO will be evaluated under the Rule of Reason, with the agencies' analysis focused on whether or not the ACO has or can exercise market power. However, the agencies will use measures of an ACO's physicians' shares within the ACO's primary service area as the measure of its market power, rather than defining relevant markets according to established antitrust law standards, and assessing market power within those markets. The *ACO Enforcement Policy Statement* also provides an antitrust safety zone for ACOs that the agencies determine do not raise market power concerns, which will assure them that they will not be the subjects of an antitrust investigation or law enforcement proceeding so long as they continue to be ACOs contracted with CMS and satisfactorily meet its program requirements.

---

[27]   *See* Federal Trade Commission and Department of Justice, Antitrust Division, Statement of Antitrust Enforcement Policy Regarding Accountable Care Organizations Participating in the Medicare Shared Savings Program, 76 Fed. Reg. 67026 (Oct. 28, 2011) (*available at* http://www.ftc.gov/opp/aco/index.shtml).

5

The Robinson-Patman Act

Stephen P. Murphy, Esquire
Edwards Wildman Palmer LLP

One of the more arcane and confusing federal antitrust laws is the federal Robinson-Patman Antidiscrimination Act, which prohibits sellers from giving and purchasers from receiving discriminatory price discounts.[1] Although traditionally the antitrust laws permit companies a fair amount of latitude to deal unilaterally with customers, Robinson-Patman limits how a seller may unilaterally differentiate prices between similarly situated customers. In addition, the Robinson-Patman Act prohibits powerful buyers from discrimination in connection with discounts exacted from sellers.

The Robinson-Patman Act prohibits price discrimination in the sale of commodities. Although the Act is not a frequent area of antitrust concern in the healthcare industry primarily because of the industry's service nature, issues generally arise with the sale of pharmaceuticals and durable medical equipment (DME). In addition, the Non-Profit Institutions Act (NPIA), which provides an exemption from Robinson-Patman, may create issues for not-for-profit hospitals that seek to allow for-profit subsidiaries, such as pharmacies or DME providers or physician clinics, to utilize supplies purchased by the hospital.

5.1 MAY A MANUFACTURER OFFER DISCOUNTS TO OUR COMPETITOR WITHOUT OFFERING US THE SAME DISCOUNTS?

The Robinson-Patman Act makes it unlawful in interstate commerce for a seller of goods to discriminate on the basis of price between purchasers of commodities of like grade and quality where the discrimination adversely effects competition.[2] The basic elements of a Robinson-Patman claim are:

- two or more sales;
- commodities sold in interstate commerce;

---

[1]   15 U.S.C. § 13.
[2]   *Id.* at § 13(a).

- different prices to similar buyers; and
- competitive injury.

5.1.1   Does the Transaction Involve a Sale of a Commodity?

As a threshold matter, the first question we must answer is whether the sale involves a commodity because the Act prohibits price discrimination only in the sale of commodities. Broadly defined, a *commodity* encompasses only tangible products, such as DME and pharmaceuticals. Services and nontangible products, such as physician or hospital services, health insurance, credit reports, and billing statements are not covered.[3] In some sections, especially in the healthcare context, services are often mixed with tangible products. An example would be a knee replacement that has a tangible component (i.e., the replacement joint) and a large service component (i.e., the surgery and hospital stay). Where there is a mix of services and goods, the courts will apply a "dominant nature of the transaction" test to determine whether the Robinson-Patman Act applies. For example, in *Kennedy Theater Ticket Service,* the district court found that even though the alleged discrimination occurred in connection with the sale of a ticket, the transaction was primarily the sale of a right to attend a performance and thus not a commodity for purposes of the Act.[4]

5.1.2   Are There Two Sales?

The second question is whether there are at least two sales—sales to both the favored and disfavored customers. Otherwise, there can be no price differential. If the manufacturer sells only to your competitor and makes you an offer but no sale, then there is no violation because there can be no discriminatory pricing.[5] In the case of an executed contract for the sale of commodities,

---

[3] *See, e.g.,* Ball Memorial Hosp. v. Mutual Hospital Insurance, 784 F.2d 1325, 1340 (7th Cir. 1986); Empire State Pharmacy Society v. Empire Blue Cross and Blue Shield, 778 F. Supp. 1253, 1258-59 (S.D.N.Y. 1991); Stand Facts Credit Services v. Experian Info. Solutions, 405 F. Supp.2d 1141, 1159 (C.D. Cal. 2005).

[4] Kennedy Theater Ticket Service, Inc. v. Ticketron, Inc., 342 F. Supp. 922, 927 (E.D. Pa. 1972).

[5] The Robinson-Patman Act requires sales by the same seller, but if a seller controls an intermediate company (e.g., a wholesaler) to the extent that it can dictate the price and terms of sale to purchasers, then the seller may still be liable under the Act for discriminatory sales. *See, e.g.* Hiram Walker, Inc. v. A & S Tropical, Inc., 407 F.2d 4, 8 (5th Cir. 1969), cert. den., 396 U.S. 901 (1969); Drug Pharm. Corp. v. American Home Prods. Corp., 472 F. Supp. 2d 385, 396 (E.D.N.Y. 2007).

some courts have held that the execution of an agreement alone can transform the *offer* into a *sale* for Robinson-Patman purposes.[6]

5.1.3   Is There a Price Difference in Similar Products?

The next question to consider is whether there is a difference in price. For Robinson-Patman purposes, the *price* is what the customer pays for the commodities after factoring in all rebates, discounts, coupons, and other allowances.[7] Thus, the comparison is one of actual net prices, which may include differences in credit and delivery terms. A variety of factors can impact the *actual net price* determination, and it may involve something more than the sticker price.[8] For example, a sale of generic acetaminophen at a price of five dollars per unit can be a discriminatory price if one customer is offered free shipping while the other is not.

When comparing the actual net prices, only contemporaneous sales are examined. The issue of contemporaneous sales is fact driven. In *LiXi v. Apple Inc.*, a Robinson-Patman class action suit alleging price discrimination in the sale of cell phones, the court held that contemporaneous sales did not occur where the sales were 14 days apart.[9] According to the court, sellers are free to change prices at any time and in any amount as long as the new price is available to all, which was the case in *LiXi*. Similarly, in *B-S Steel of Kansas, Inc. v. Texas Industries, Inc.*, the court found that purchases separated by five months were not "reasonably contemporaneous."[10]

Finally, the commodities sold at different prices must be of like grade and quality. If the commodities' differences are only in warranties or packaging, then they are still of like grade and quality.[11] The Supreme Court affirmed a conclusion by the Federal Trade Commission (FTC) in *Borden*

---

[6]   *See* Harper Plastics, Inc. v. Amoco Chemicals Corp., 615 F. 2d 468, 471 (7th Cir. 1980); Aluminum Co. of America v. Tandet, 235 F. Supp. 111, 114 (D. Conn. 1964).

[7]   Thomas J. Kline, Inc. v. Lorillard, Inc., 878 F.2d 791, 794 (4th Cir. 1989); Rose Confections Inc. v. Ambrosia Chocolate Co., 816 F.2d 381, 387 (8th Cir. 1987).

[8]   *See, e.g.*, Raynor Manufacturing Co., v. Raynor Door Co., 2009 U.S. Dist. LEXIS 6159 (D. Kan. 2009); Video Services of America v. Maxell Corp. of America, 2007 U.S. Dist. LEXIS 54107 (D.N.J. 2007); Conoco Inc. v. Inman Oil, 774 F.2d 895, 901–02 (8th Cir. 1985).

[9]   603 F. Supp.2d 464, 471 (E.D.N.Y. 2009).

[10]   439 F.3d 653, 665 (10th Cir. 2006). *See* Atalanta Trading Corp. v. FTC, 258 F.2d 365, 371 (2d Cir. 1958) (seven-month interval between sales not contemporaneous). *But see* Inomed Labs. LLC v. Alza Corp., 2002-2 Trade Cases (CCH) ¶ 73, 876 at 95,220 (S.D.N.Y. 2002) (contracts separated by "a few months" contemporaneous).

[11]   *E.g.*, DeLong Equip. v. Washington Mills Abrasion, 887 F.2d 1499, 1517 (11th Cir. 1989).

that branded and nonbranded evaporated milk were still of like grade and quality despite the fact that the branded product commanded a higher price and greater consumer preference—"mere labels" were not enough to differentiate the products.[12] Setting aside labels, the critical inquiry is on the "characteristics of the product themselves" in determining like grade and quality.[13] If there are, however, real physical differences in the branded and nonbranded products that can affect marketability, then such products likely are not of "like grade and quality."[14]

5.1.4 Did the Sales Occur in Interstate Commerce?

At least one of the sales must be in interstate, as opposed to intrastate, commerce. The Robinson-Patman Act requires that the commodities in at least one such sale actually cross a state line.[15] This requirement is unlike the typical interstate commerce requirement where the sale simply must affect interstate commerce. Thus, purely intrastate[16] or purely foreign[17] sales are not subject to the Robinson-Patman Act.

5.1.5 Is There Competitive Injury, and If So, at What Level?

Proof of actual competitive injury is not required in a price discrimination case under Robinson-Patman. There need only be a "reasonable possibility" of an injury to competition. Indeed, the type of proof required differs considerably depending on whether or not the buyer is a seller's competitor.

Determining competitive injury under the Act involves an analysis of the parties' relationships to each other. This, perhaps, is one of the more peculiar aspects of a Robinson-Patman analysis as it differs substantially from the analysis of competitive effects in other antitrust cases. The courts have used the labels primary, secondary, or tertiary line injury to identify the relationships between the parties and the type of injury involved. Whether the injury is deemed primary, secondary, or tertiary determines the amount of proof required.

---

[12] FTC v. Borden Co., 383 U.S. 637, 639–47 (1966).

[13] *Id.* at 638.

[14] *See* Utah Foam Prods. v. Upjohn, 154 F. 3d 1212, 1217–18 (10th Cir. 1998).

[15] Gulf Oil Corp. v. Copp Paving Co., 419 U.S. 186, 195 (1974).

[16] Lucas v. Citizens Communications Co., 2007 U.S. App. LEXIS 15578 (9th Cir. 2007).

[17] General Chems. v. Exxon Chem. Co., U.S.A., 625 F.2d 1231, 1234 (5th Cir. 1980).

5.1.5.1 Primary Line Injury: Predatory Pricing

A *primary line violation* involves discrimination in price that affects the discriminating seller's direct competitors. Primary line competitive injury is akin to a claim of predatory pricing injury under Section 2 of the Sherman Antitrust Act. That is, a primary line injury requires a showing of pricing below some level of costs and a "dangerous probability" of recoupment.

The leading primary line price discrimination case is *Brooke Group Ltd. v. Brown & Williamson Tobacco Corp.*[18] The plaintiff, Liggett, was a producer of generic, unbranded "black and white" cigarettes. Liggett alleged that the defendant, a producer of branded cigarettes, entered the generic market and discounted, substantially, its prices to the plaintiff's primary wholesalers to drive generic cigarettes out of the market. Liggett further alleged the defendant believed that the generic manufacturer would be unable to match the defendant's price discount. Although a jury returned a verdict in favor of the plaintiff, the trial court granted judgment as matter of law for the defendant. The trial court's decision was ultimately affirmed by the Supreme Court.

In its decision, the Supreme Court noted that, in the 25 years since *Utah Pie*,[19] exploration of the law had revealed that primary line competitive injury under the Robinson-Patman Act was similar to and should be analyzed under the same framework as that applied to predatory pricing injury actionable under the Sherman Act, Section 2. Accordingly, for primary line discount cases to be actionable, the plaintiff must provide clear proof of anticompetitive harm in the form of below-cost pricing—i.e., "pricing below an appropriate measure of its rival's cost"[20] —with an object to eliminate competitors and a "dangerous probability" of recoupment—that is, being able to charge higher prices to recoup its lost monopoly rents after driving the generic manufacturers from the market.[21]

5.1.5.2 Secondary Line Discrimination: Lost Profits

A secondary line violation involves discrimination in price between the seller's competing customers that injures competition between them. A prima facie case of secondary line price discrimination occurs when a seller charges different prices to competing customers, and the effect of the price discrimination is to injure competition to the benefit of the favored customer. The requisite competitive injury may be inferred when there is substantial price

---

[18]   509 U.S. 209 (1993).

[19]   Utah Pie Co. v. Continental Baking Co., 386 U.S. 685 (1967).

[20]   Brooke Group Ltd. v. Brown & Williamson Tobacco Corp., 509 U.S. at 222.

[21]   *Id.* at 224.

discrimination between customers who compete and such discrimination is sustained over a significant period of time.[22] For this analysis to be applicable, there must be actual competition between the customers and a diversion from the disfavored to the favored customer of profits or sales.[23] The discrimination must be "substantial" as a small or de minimus price discrimination does not create a viable claim.

To establish secondary line injury, the plaintiff must show that it was actually injured. Evidence of actual lost sales or profits due to the alleged discrimination can prove such injury, but it is far more typical to make the requisite showing through an inference. In *FTC v. Morton Salt*,[24] the Supreme Court permitted an inference of injury to be drawn where there was a substantial discrimination in price involving a product for resale, the price discrimination occurred over a substantial time period, and competition between the two buyers was "keen."[25] The majority of cases permits the requisite injury finding where only one competitor is injured. This differs from the traditional antitrust analysis that requires injury to the competitive process itself, and injury to one competitor usually is not sufficient to establish an antitrust claim.

5.1.5.3   Tertiary Line Discrimination: Crossing the Border

The language of Section 2(a) of the Robinson-Patman Act also provides a remedy for *tertiary line violations*, which occur when there is a price discrimination that affects customers of the favored and disfavored secondary line customers. In *Texaco Inc. v. Hasbrouck*,[26] the disfavored customers were independent Texaco retailers who competed in the retail market with two companies who also were distributors for Texaco and, as such, received substantial discounts on their gasoline purchases. The Supreme Court found the requisite injury because the distributors' significant discount was not tied to the distributors' actual costs of marketing, hauling, or storing the gasoline, or of any actual savings to Texaco.[27] Tertiary line cases are unlikely to be litigated because of a lack of a relationship between the seller and downstream purchaser and a lack of significant injury. A difficulty with tertiary line liability is that it can also interfere with legitimate antitrust goals of allowing the

---

[22]   *See, e.g.,* Volvo Trucks North America v. Reeder-Simco GMC, Inc., 546 U.S. 164, 177 (2006).

[23]   *Id. See* Feesers, Inc. v. Michael Foods, Inc., 591 F.3d 191, 213–14 (3d Cir. 2010); Camarda v. Snapple Distributors, 2007 U.S. Dist. LEXIS 68101 (S.D.N.Y. 2007).

[24]   334 U.S. 37 (1948).

[25]   *Id.* at 50–51.

[26]   496 U.S. 543 (1990).

[27]   *Id.* at 559–571. *See also,* Perkins v. Standard Oil Co., 395 U.S. 642 (1969).

resellers' freedom in pricing decisions at all levels of distribution. Tertiary line discrimination should be actionable only where the seller has some type of control over its customer's customer, and there is evidence that the original discrimination actually caused the tertiary line injury.

5.1.6   Defenses to a Robinson-Patman Claim

Even if all of the elements of a prima facie price discrimination claim are met, the Robinson-Patman Act permits application of a series of defenses to avoid liability.

5.1.6.1   Meeting Competition

The first defense, provided by Section 2(b) of the Robinson-Patman Act, is for "meeting competition" where a seller acts "in good faith to meet an equally low price of a competitor."[28] The defense of *meeting competition* is available in two situations: first, where the seller, in giving the discount, is meeting competition from another seller and, second, where the seller is, in reducing its price, assisting the buyer in meeting its competition. In the first case, the seller must be able to demonstrate "the existence of facts which would lead a reasonable and prudent person to believe that the granting of a lower price would, in fact, meet the equally low price of a competitor."[29] The best scenario for establishing a meeting competition defense is through systematic documentation of evidence, typically from customers, that a lower price was in response to a competitor.[30] A best practice in this situation is to have standardized forms that are required to be systematically prepared, veri-fied (if possible), and maintained so that, if a price is claimed as discrimina-tory, the defense can be sustained. The seller's failure to engage in this type of good faith confirmation of a meeting competition situation can lead a court to reject the defense.[31] A significant pitfall in establishing a meeting competition defense is that it would be highly problematic for the seller to contact its com-petitors for price verification, as that could lead to a Sherman Act violation.[32] The defense is not limited to one-on-one localized competitive situations— area-wide (even state-wide) meeting competition pricing can be used if there is adequate evidence to support it.

---

[28]   Standard Oil Co. v. F.T.C., 340 U.S. 231, 251 (1951).

[29]   United States v. United States Gypsum Co., 438 U.S. 422, 451 (1978).

[30]   *Id.* at 455. *See, e.g.,* Bristol Steel & Iron Works v. Bethlehem Steel Corp., 41 F.3d 182, 188 (4th Cir. 1992).

[31]   Hoover Color Corp. v. Bayer Corp., 199 F.3d 160, 165-67 (4th Cir. 1999).

[32]   United States Gypsum, 438 U.S. at 453–59. *See* 15 U.S.C. Sec. 1.

For the defense potentially to apply to a customer's efforts to meet competition, the customer's competitor must be vertically integrated *or* the competitor must have received a discount from a supplier.[33] The FTC has accepted both of these factors as exceptions to the general requirement that the customers be competitors for purposes of the meeting competition defense.[34]

5.1.6.2   Cost Justification

The next defense to a Robinson-Patman price discrimination claim is the *cost justification* defense in which price differences are permitted that "make only due allowance for differences in the cost of manufacture, sale, or delivery resulting from the differing methods or quantities" for which products are "sold or delivered."[35] There are a wide variety of costs that can qualify under the defense including distribution, delivery, selling, manufacturing, billing and credit loss, catalogue, warranty, and advertising costs. In *United States v. Borden Co.*, the Court recognized the difficulty of a customer-by-customer cost justification and adopted a cost justification defense on a group buyer basis, assuming "selfsameness" among the buyers—i.e., a "close resemblance of the individual members of each group on the essential point or points which determine the costs considered."[36]

Unfortunately, courts and the FTC require actual cost evidence to satisfy the cost justification defense. A seller must demonstrate actual cost savings equal to or greater than the price discrimination to quality for the defense.[37] Understandably, this heavy evidentiary burden has curtailed substantially the use of the defense.

5.1.6.3   Changing Conditions

The next defense to a Robinson-Patman claim is the *changing conditions* defense in which the change must be dire—imminent deterioration of perishable goods, obsolescence of seasonal goods, court-ordered distress sales, or discontinuance of business.[38] Sellers can qualify for this defense if they are reacting to an industry-wide crisis or where they are reacting to a crisis in their own goods' marketability.[39] This defense is potentially applicable

---

[33]   FTC v. Sun Oil Co., 371 U.S. 505, 512 n.7 (1963).

[34]   *See* FTC Statement of Commission Policy with Respect to Anticompetitive Practices in the Marketing of Gasoline (June 30, 1967).

[35]   15 U.S.C. § 13(a).

[36]   370 U.S. 460, 469 (1962).

[37]   *See, e.g.,* FTC v. Morton Salt Co., 334 U.S. 37, 48 (1948).

[38]   *See* 15 U.S.C. § 13(a).

[39]   *Id.*

beyond the changes in marketability listed in the statute, but the courts have been reluctant to step beyond the specific examples.

5.1.6.4   Functional Availability

The last defense is based on functional availability. The courts have construed this defense from the intent, but not the language, of Section 2(a) of the Robinson-Patman Act, by incorporating the defense from the availability requirement of Sections 2(d) and (e) of the Act. The *functional availability* defense requires two showings. First, the disfavored buyer must have knowledge of the lower price's availability. Second, many competing customers must be able to obtain the lower price; availability must be real, not theoretical.

Where a meaningful number of customers are unable to purchase enough of a seller's products to qualify for volume discounts, then there is no functional availability.[40] Where, however, buyers only need to rearrange their marketing schemes to qualify for a market share discount, then the price discount is functionally available and does not violate the Robinson-Patman Act.[41]

With careful attention to the detailed burden of proof required for these defenses, a commodities' seller can offer discriminatory pricing to favored customers.

5.2   MAY A NOT-FOR-PROFIT HOSPITAL PROVIDE PHARMACEUTICALS TO ITS PATIENTS FOR USE OUTSIDE THE HOSPITAL WITHOUT VIOLATING THE ROBINSON-PATMAN ACT?

Under the NPIA, not-for-profit institutions are exempt from the Robinson-Patman Act, for "purchases of their supplies for their own use."[42] The NPIA has been found to apply in a variety of situations:

- to exempt an HMO's purchase and resale to HMO members of pharmaceuticals[43]
- to exempt a hospital's purchase of pharmaceuticals for resale to the hospital's nonprofit parent's employees[44]

---

[40]   FTC v. Morton Salt Co., 334 U.S. 37 (1948).

[41]   Smith Wholesale Co. v. R.J. Reynolds Tobacco Co., 477 F.3d 854 (6th Cir. 2007).

[42]   15 U.S.C. § 13.

[43]   *See* DC Moderna v. Kaiser Foundation Health Plans, 743 F.2d 1388 (9th Cir. 1984).

[44]   *See* FTC Advisory Opinion to BJC Health Systems, 1999 WL 3349-799 (Nov. 9, 1999).

- to exempt a school district's purchases of pharmaceuticals for school district employees dispensed through local pharmacies[45]
- to exempt a university's purchase of pharmaceuticals for its employee health plan[46]

For nonprofit hospitals, this exemption has been held to apply to a hospital's purchase and resale of pharmaceuticals to the "inpatient, or to the emergency facility patient, upon his discharge for his personal use [of pharmaceutical products] away from [hospital] premises" and to the "outpatient for personal use away from the premises."[47] These prescriptions sales are generally intended for a limited time period as an extension of treatment provided at the hospital.[48] The exemption is, however, not unlimited. It does not extend to refills of pharmaceutical product prescriptions for a former patient.[49] Although a patient's pharmaceutical product's continued use may be medically indicated, the prescription refill, being beyond a "limited take-home prescription," is not a pharmaceutical purchase for the hospital's "own use." Exceeding the scope of own use exceeds the scope of the NPIA exemption.

5.3   CAN NONPROFIT AND FOR-PROFIT AFFILIATE CORPORATIONS IN THE SAME HEALTH NETWORK SHARE PRODUCTS PURCHASED BY THE NOT-FOR-PROFIT ENTITY WITHOUT VIOLATING THE ROBINSON-PATMAN ACT?

The NPIA exempts from the Robinson-Patman Act "purchases of . . . supplies for their own use by schools, colleges, universities, public libraries, churches, hospitals, and charitable institutions not operated for profit."[50] Under this statute, "mere participation" by a for-profit corporation in an arrangement to provide healthcare services does not void the exemption.[51] When a

---

[45] *See* FTC Staff Advisory Opinion to Alpena Public Schools (June 16, 2006) (*available at* www.ftc.gov/os/2006/061606Alpena.pdf).

[46] *See* FTC Staff Advisory Opinion to University of Michigan (Apr. 9, 2010) (*available at* www.ftc.gov/opa/2010/04/npia.shtm).

[47] Abbott Laboratories, Inc. v. Portland Retail Druggists Association, Inc., 425 U.S. 1, 2, 15–16 (1976).

[48] *Id.,* at 15.

[49] *Id.,* at 15–16.

[50] 15 U.S.C. § 13c.

[51] *See* Letter from Marcus H. Meier (Federal Trade Commission) to Robert E. Block at 14 (Feb. 13, 2008) (*available at* http//www.ftc.gov/bc/adops/08 0213 Kaiser.pdf).

nonprofit is purchasing supplies, which it in turn is sharing with a for-profit corporate affiliate, the fact that the nonprofit purchases the supplies potentially allows for application of the NPIA exemption to the purchase. However, if any of the financial benefits from the not-for-profit's purchase inures to the benefit of the for-profit, the exemption can be lost.

In an April 9, 2010, advisory letter, the FTC's Health Care Division opined that a public university's prescription drug benefit program would fall within the scope of an NPIA exemption, even though for-profit entities were involved.[52] The FTC found that the role of the for-profit entities would be "limited" and that they would not enjoy any financial advantage from the NPIA supplies; thus, the FTC permitted the exemption. Sharing of the NPIA-exempted supplies by a nonprofit purchaser with a for-profit affiliate can, therefore, cause loss of the exemption if the sharing permits the for-profit to enjoy financial advantages over non-NITA–exempted supplies.

Resources

Brooke Group v. Brown & Williamson Tobacco Group, 509 U.S. 209 (1993).

Federal Trade Commission Guide to the Antitrust Laws: Price Discrimination Among Buyers (available at www.ftc.gov/bc/antitrust/price_discrimination. shtm).

FTC v. Borden Co., 383 U.S. 637 (1966).

Volvo Trucks North America v. Reeder-Simco GMC, Inc., 546 US. 164 (2006).

See DeModena v. Kaiser Foundation Health Plan, Inc., 743 F.2d 1388, 1391–1392 (9th Cir. 1984).

[52] *See* Letter from Markus H. Meier (Federal Trade Commission) to Kathleen A. Reed (Apr. 9, 2010) (*available at* http/www.ftc.gov/os/2010/04/index.shtm).

6

Healthcare Payer Issues

Patricia M. Wagner, Esquire
Epstein Becker & Green PC

Contracts between health plans and providers raise a number of negotiation points between the parties. As discussed below, provisions that present a business opportunity for one or both parties may raise antitrust risks or concerns. More important, the risk can arise even if the parties to the agreement are satisfied with the terms. Challenges can be raised by excluded competitors, competitors who believe they have been harmed by the contractual provisions, and by federal and state antitrust enforcement agencies. The costs of defending such a challenge can be considerable even when the challenge is unjustified. The questions below highlight some contractual provisions that may raise antitrust concerns, particularly in cases where one or both of the parties have significant market power.

6.1   WHEN ARE MOST FAVORED NATION PROVISIONS ILLEGAL UNDER THE ANTITRUST LAWS?

Whether a most favored nation (MFN) provision is legal under the antitrust laws is dependent on the market power of the buyer and the likely effect that an MFN will have on prices in the relevant market. The question is whether the MFN will cause prices to increase (harming consumers) or diminish the ability of competitors to constrain the buyer's market power.

An MFN provision generally is an agreement imposed by a buyer that states that the seller may charge the buyer no more than the lowest price it charges to any other buyer. In some cases, an MFN provision may require that the seller charge the buyer a certain percentage less than any other buyer.

Some states have explicitly legislated against inclusion of MFN provisions in contracts between health plans and hospitals or providers. For example, Ohio prohibits a payer from including an MFN in a contract with a hospital or with a provider other than a hospital.[1]

---

[1]   Ohio Rev. Code Ann. §3963.11, the provision becomes effective in 2011; Other states have similar prohibitions, *see e.g.*, NH Rev. Stat. §417:4 (the insurance code that defines as an unfair method of competition and unfair and deceptive acts and practices

MFNs may be challenged under the Sherman Act under Section 1 as an unreasonable restraint of trade or Section 2 as a monopoly or attempt to monopolize.[2] Generally, MFNs have been challenged by the Department of Justice (DOJ).[3] However, the Federal Trade Commission (FTC) and State Attorneys General have brought enforcement actions against parties (mostly insurers) with contractual MFNs as well.[4] On a few occasions, private parties have challenged these arrangements under the argument that the existence of the MFN prevented them from obtaining discounts necessary to compete. In addition, the announcement of a DOJ investigation or complaint alleging the anticompetitive use of an MFN can be followed by private actions.[5]

In the usual case, the MFN will have the potential to violate the antitrust laws if: (1) The buyer extracting the MFN provision has market power, (2) the buyer represents a substantial share of the sellers' income, and (3) a high percentage of sellers (or a seller with significant market power) are bound to the MFN. In that situation, the *theory of competitive harm* is that the sellers will be discouraged from giving larger discounts to other buyers, as the financial impact of doing so would be too significant. As a result, smaller buyers are charged higher prices, and the price to consumers increases and/or other buyers are foreclosed from effectively competing in the market (because their costs are higher and, therefore, their prices are higher than the dominant buyer).

In this regard, the enforcement agencies have alleged Sherman Act violations against managed care organizations with market power. The MFN clauses imposed by managed care organization in combination with the existence of market power prevents the supplier from providing a lower price

---

"using or enforcing any 'most favored nation' or 'equally favored nation' provision in any contract for medical care provider services."); RI. Gen. Laws §23-17.13-3 ("a health plan shall not include a most favored rate clause in a provider contract").

[2] *See e.g.*, U.S. v. Blue Cross Blue Shield of Michigan, Civil Action No. 2:10-cv-15155-DPH-MKM, *available at* http://www.justice.gov/atr/cases/f263200/263235. htm (case brought under Section 1 of the Sherman Act); Ocean State Physicians Health Plan, Inc. v. Blue Cross Blue Shield of Rhode Island, 883 F.2d 1101 (1st Cir. 1989) (case brought under Section 2 of the Sherman Act).

[3] *See e.g.*, U.S. v. Blue Cross Blue Shield of Michigan, Civil Action No. 2:10-cv-15155-DPH-MKM, *available at* http://www.justice.gov/atr/cases/f263200/263235. htm; U.S. v. Medical Mutual of Ohio, 1999-1 Trade Cas. (CCH) 72,465 (N.D. Ohio 1999); United States and State of Arizona v. Delta Dental Plan of Arizona, Inc., Civ. No. 94-1793 PHXPGR (D. Ariz. August 30, 1994).

[4] In re RxCare of Tennessee, Inc., 121 F.T.C. 762 (1996); *see also* investigation by Connecticut Attorney General *available at* www.ct.gov/ag/cwp/view. asp?A=2341&Q=454688.

[5] *See* Aetna, Inc. v. Blue Cross Blue Shield of Michigan, Civil Action No. 2:11-cv-15346-DPH-MKM (filed December 6, 2011).

(greater discount) to any other managed care organization. The argument is that the supplier/provider (physician and/or hospital) cannot afford to provide the same, lower price to the managed care organization with market power that has imposed the MFN provision.

In contrast, if the managed care plan does not have market power, the MFN arguably has procompetitive effects. Specifically, it can only ensure a nondominant purchaser the lowest possible price, without the offsetting anticompetitive effect of prohibiting lower discounts to others, precisely because the purchaser is not large enough to force the establishment of a floor on discounts.

The DOJ has taken a more expansive view of how an MFN provision can be anticompetitive and generally brings such actions under Section 1 of the Sherman Act. Recently, the DOJ brought an action against Blue Cross Blue Shield of Michigan alleging that the MFN policies of Blue Cross Blue Shield of Michigan violated Section 1 of the Sherman Act.[6] In its complaint, DOJ alleges that Blue Cross Blue Shield of Michigan implemented hospital contracts that required 22 hospitals "to charge some or all other commercial insurers *more* than the hospital charges Blue Cross, typically by a specified percentage differential." The complaint further alleged that in some cases, these so-called "MFN-plus" clauses resulted in a differential of as much as 40 percent.[7] In addition, DOJ alleges that Blue Cross Blue Shield of Michigan instituted MFN clauses with other hospitals under which the hospitals would charge other payers at least as much as they charged Blue Cross. A hospital that did not accept this MFN "would be paid approximately 16 percent less by Blue Cross than if it accepts the MFN."[8] The DOJ's complaint alleges that such conduct has had anticompetitive effects including raising prices to consumers and restricting or limiting entry and expansion by competitor health plans.[9] The respondent's motion to dismiss in that case was denied.[10]

Similarly, in *United States and State of Arizona v. Delta Dental Plan of Arizona, Inc.,* the DOJ alleged that an MFN imposed by Delta Dental Plan of Arizona eliminated discounts and reduced price competition.[11] There, the DOJ alleged that the agreement had the effect of preventing dentists from

---

[6] *See e.g.,* U.S. v. Blue Cross Blue Shield of Michigan, Civil Action No. 2:10-cv-15155-DPH-MKM, *available at* http://www.justice.gov/atr/cases/f263200/263235.htm.

[7] *Id.*

[8] *Id.*

[9] *Id.*

[10] U.S. v. Blue Cross Blue Shield of Michigan, __F.Supp.2d__2011 WL 3566486 (E.D. Mich. 2011).

[11] Civ. No. 94-1793 PHXPGR (D. Ariz. August 30, 1994).

cutting fees below those offered in the Delta Plan. Approximately 85 percent of the dentists in the alleged relevant geographic market contract with the Delta Plan. The DOJ alleged that prior to the Delta Plan's enforcement of the MFN, many of the dentists provided discounts to payers 25 to 40 percent off of charges. After the Delta Plan instituted the MFN, DOJ alleged that hundreds of dentists who had signed up with other competitor dental plans were forced to resign from those plans.[12] In a public statement regarding the case, the then Assistant Attorney General of the Antitrust Division stated "[T]he use of the most favored nation clause by Delta facilitated anticompetitive behavior by reducing or eliminating discounts and limiting competition."[13] The DOJ indicated that because "so many Arizona dentists participate in the Delta Plan, and because Delta patients account for a significant part of the dentists' income, the [MFN clauses] . . . have led many dentists to stop discounting and severely restricted competing dental plans' ability to attract and retain enough dentists to serve their members."[14]

In *U.S. v. Medical Mutual of Ohio,* the DOJ alleged that Medical Mutual of Ohio violated Section 1 of the Sherman Act by including a "most favorable rates requirement" with participating hospitals.[15] The DOJ alleged that the provision: (1) Required hospitals to charge Medical Mutual's competitors who had less volume at least as much as they charged Medical Mutual's indemnity product allegedly creating a price differential of 15 to 20 percent between Medical Mutual's managed care products and competitors' managed care products. (2) Another requirement forced hospitals to charge all health plans 1 to 10 percent more than those hospitals charged for the Medical Mutual's indemnity product. (3) Even when Medical Mutual agreed to similar product clauses that would compare rates between product lines, it still required hospitals to charge 10 to 15 percent more to any health plan that provided less volume to a hospital than did Medical Mutual.

The DOJ alleged that Medical Mutual's contractual provision increased the cost of hospital service and health insurance for businesses and consumers in the Cleveland area. In addition, the DOJ alleged that by enforcing the MFN without any regard to differences in products, patient mix, case management, and contracting methodologies, the provision stifled creative contractual arrangements between payers and hospitals, deterred development of

---

[12] Competitive impact statement, *available at* http://www.justice.gov/atr/cases/f205400/205401.htm.

[13] Statement of Anne Bingham, *available at* http://www.justice.gov/opa/pr/Pre_96/August94/azdental.txt.html.

[14] Competitive Impact Statement, *available at* http://www.justice.gov/atr/cases/f205400/205401.htm.

[15] 1999-1 Trade Cas. (CCH) 72,465 (N.D. Ohio 1999).

innovative health plans, and hindered the growth of less-costly health plans. In that case, the DOJ alleged that Medical Mutual's market share in the commercial insurance market was roughly 36 percent, and accounted for between 25 to 30 percent of commercial insurance revenue to hospitals; stating that "nearly all [of the local hospitals] depend on Medical Mutual for the largest share of their commercial business."[16]

The DOJ is reasonably successful in obtaining consent decrees against the MFNs it has challenged. To date, in the situations where the DOJ's challenge was resisted, the court, preliminarily, ruled in favor of the DOJ.[17] However, in general, courts have been less willing to find an MFN provision as anticompetitive and violative of the antitrust laws. For example, in *Ocean State Physicians Health Plan, Inc. v. Blue Cross & Blue Shield of Rhode Island*, Blue Cross had instituted a policy known as the *Prudent Buyer policy*, which stated that Blue Cross would not pay a physician any more for a service than that physician was paid for the service by Ocean State; a Blue Cross competitor.[18] The case was brought under Section 2 of the Sherman Act, and the court held that, despite the fact that Blue Cross had monopoly power, the conduct did not violate the Section 2 prohibition against monopolization. Similarly, in *Kitsap Physicians Service v. Washington Dental Service,* an MFN provision was challenged under Section 2 as an attempted monopolization.[19] The court found the MFN provision acceptable, noting that the clause provided insurance companies protection from being overcharged by the dentists and from being priced out of the dental insurance market. Significantly, there the court found that the defendant's market share was only 13 percent and, therefore, not enough to give rise to a dangerous probability of attempted monopolization.

In sum, to determine whether an MFN might be viewed as anticompetitive requires an analysis of the buyer's market power, the market power of the seller, or the number of sellers to which the MFN will apply. The obvious question is when a buyer's market power will be sufficient to raise concern. Although there is no hard and fast answer, given the DOJ's past enforcement activity, it may be wise to evaluate the potential effects of an MFN provision any time the buyer's market power is greater than 30 percent of the relevant market. In some cases, the potential risk alone may deter the parties from

---

[16]   Competitive Impact Statement, *available at* http://www.justice.gov/atr/cases/f1900/1958.htm.

[17]   U.S. v. Blue Cross Blue Shield of Michigan, __F.Supp.2d__ 2011 WL 3566486 (E.D. Mich. 2011) (case still pending); U.S. v. Delta Dental of Rhode Island, 943 F. Supp. 172 (D. R.I. 1996) (at that point, the respondent entered into a consent decree).

[18]   883 F.2d 1101 (1st Cir. 1989).

[19]   671 F. Supp. 1267 (W.D. Wash. 1987).

including such a provision, while others may be comfortable that proposed benefits of the arrangement (or lack of competitive harm) will be sufficient to dissuade, at most, a brief scrutiny that will escape any challenge.

6.2 THE DOMINANT PAYER WILL NOT AGREE TO OUR REASONABLE RATE INCREASES. WHAT CAN WE DO?

The answer depends on whether the provider is acting in its own unilateral interest or is attempting to act in concert with other competing providers. A group boycott arises if competitors agree (again, either explicitly or implicitly) with each other that they will not deal with a payer unless the payer meets certain terms. A "classic boycott involves concerted action with a purpose either to exclude a person or group from the market, or to accomplish some other anticompetitive object, or both."[20] "[C]ommercially motivated group boycotts, or concerted refusals to deal, generally are considered illegal *per se* under Section 1."[21] "The *per se* rules can result in erroneous conclusions in some cases, but '[f]or the sake of business certainty and litigation efficiency, we have tolerated the invalidation of some agreements that a fullblown inquiry might have proved to be reasonable.'"[22]

There are two elements to a *per se* illegal boycott under Section 1 of the Sherman Act, "(1) at least some of the boycotters were competitors of each other and the target, and (2) the boycott was designed to protect the boycotters from competition with the target."[23]

In other words, competing providers should not coordinate action to force a dominant payer to negotiate on special terms or at special rates. If the provider is acting unilaterally, the provider may make the decision not to contract with the dominant payer. Forcing a payer to accept other terms may be difficult, however, as a payer is not obligated to contract with every provider and is not obligated to contract on the provider's terms.

However, a buyer (such as a payer) with significant market power may have monopsony power. Where monopoly power relates to the power of a particular seller in a market, *monopsony power* relates to the power of a particular purchaser in a market. As is true of monopoly power, monopsony

---

[20] Armstrong Surgical Ctr. v. Armstrong County Mem'l Hosp., 185 F.3d 154, 157 (3d Cir. 1999).

[21] *See* Fed. Trade Comm'n v. Superior Court Trial Lawyers Ass'n, 493 U.S. 411, 431-32 (1990); Weiss v. York Hosp., 745 F.2d 786, 818 (3d Cir. 1984).

[22] North Texas Specialty Physicians v. F.T.C., 528 F.3d 346, 360 (5th Cir. 2008) (*quoting* Arizona v. Maricopa County Med. Soc., 457 U.S. 332, 344 (1982).

[23] Cathedral Trading, LLC v. Chicago Bd. Options Exchange, 199 F. Supp. 2d 851, 859 (N.D. Ill. 2002).

power requires a certain level of market share. The level of monopsony power is significant because the antitrust risks increase as the monopsony power increases. Whether monoposony power is being abused is evaluated similarly to whether monopoly power is being abused. Refusing to agree to rate increases may not be sufficient to raise anticompetitive concerns; however, if such conduct is combined with other conduct (such as a demand for exclusive contract or an MFN provision), the conduct might raise antitrust risk.

For example, where a purchaser has significant market power, the presence of exclusive contracts could create antitrust risks. Typically, exclusive contracts raise anticompetitive concerns if they foreclose a significant amount of competitors from the market. In some cases, contracts that offer preferential pricing can be considered exclusive contracts. Similarly, discounts that are dependent on exclusivity can create antitrust concerns when there is a dominant payer that can force a provider to make an all or nothing choice. In general, such arrangements are not *per se* illegal under the antitrust laws, but may be deemed illegal if they result in anticompetitive effects. In *Tampa Electric*, the Supreme Court explained that, in evaluating exclusive arrangements, a court should

> weigh the probable effect of the contract on the relevant area of effective competition, taking into account the relative strength of the parties, the proportionate volume of commerce involved in relation to the total volume of commerce in the relevant market area, and the probable immediate and future effects which pre-emption of that share of the market might have on effective competition therein.[24]

Exclusive contracts become an antitrust concern when exercised by a firm with significant market power because that firm can foreclose a significant amount of competition. While case law is not clear on just how much foreclosure is needed before an exclusive arrangement raises antitrust concerns, courts have indicated that for a Section 1 violation, foreclosure levels of less than 30 to 40 percent are unlikely to raise antitrust concerns. There is some case law that suggests that under Section 2, the level of foreclosure created by contract foreclosure may be lower, but only if there is a dangerous probability that the organization may achieve monopoly power as a result of the foreclosure.

---

[24] Tampa Elec. Co. v. Nashville Co., 365 U.S. 320, 328–29 (1961); see also, U.S. Healthcare, Inc. v. Healthsource, Inc., 986 F.2d 589, 595 (1st Cir. 1993) ("[t]o condemn such arrangements after *Tampa* requires a detailed depiction of circumstances and the most careful weighing of alleged dangers and potential benefits, which is to say the normal treatment afforded by the rule of reason."); *see also,* Stop & Shop Supermarket Co., v. Blue Cross & Blue Shield of Rhode Island, 373 F.3d 57, 62 (1st Cir. 2004).

In sum, a provider can act unilaterally to negotiate better terms with a payer or refuse to contract with a payer. Indeed, in some cases a provider may suggest that it will give the payer better (lower) rates if the contract is exclusive to the provider. In general, such conduct will not raise antitrust scrutiny. However, independent providers acting in concert will always raise antitrust concerns. In addition, although exclusive arrangements are generally acceptable, when the exclusive arrangement will foreclose a significant amount of competition, it, too, could raise antitrust concerns.

6.3 THE LOCAL TERTIARY HEALTHCARE SYSTEM INSISTS ON A SIGNIFICANT RATE INCREASE. IS THIS AN ANTITRUST VIOLATION?

Just as buyers can choose to deal with whom they want, sellers have a similar choice. Even if the local tertiary healthcare system has significant market power, the request for increased rates is not necessarily actionable under the antitrust laws.

Monopoly power is often defined as "the power to control prices or exclude competition."[25] Essentially, it is nothing more than a high degree of *market power*, which is the power to price profitably above competitive levels.[26] Monopoly power "may be proven directly by evidence of the control of prices or the exclusion of competition, or it may be inferred from one firm's large percentage share of the relevant market."[27]

Antitrust law does not prohibit obtaining or maintaining a monopoly through "growth or development as a consequence of a superior product, business acumen, or historic accident."[28] On the other hand, the Sherman Act does place limitations on the ways in which a firm can obtain, maintain, or use its monopoly power, or the ways in which the firm increases market power so that there is a dangerous probability that the market power will turn into monopoly power. If the creation or maintenance of monopoly power is a result of conduct unrelated to producing a superior product, the conduct could be legally actionable.

"'Anticompetitive conduct' can come in too many different forms, and is too dependent upon context, for any court or commentator ever to have

---

[25] United States v. Grinnell Corp., 384 U.S. 563 at 571 (citations omitted).
[26] Tops Markets, Inc. v. Quality Markets, Inc., 142 F. 3d 90, 97 (2d Cir. 1998).
[27] Tops Mkts., 142 F.3d at 98.
[28] United States v. Grinnell Corp., et al, 384 U.S. 563, 571 (1966).

enumerated all the varieties."[29] "The challenge for an antitrust court lies in stating a general rule for distinguishing between exclusionary acts, which reduce social welfare, and competitive acts, which increase it."[30]

Conduct that is demonstrably anticompetitive, either because it increases market power or results in direct evidence of anticompetitive effects should be presumed predatory unless the defendant proffers a valid "pro-competitive justification" for its conduct.[31] It is not clear that the request for higher rates, on its own, would be sufficient to trigger antitrust liability.

However, if the local hospital system is able to request the increase in rates as a result of a recent merger or acquisition, the conduct might be actionable. Mergers and acquisitions violate Section 7 of the Clayton Act if they increase market power, and the exercise of that added market power raises price and/or excludes competition. The theory is that a merged entity is able to raise price because the merger increases market power, and the increase in market power is not offset by efficiencies that benefit consumers by making the market more, rather than less, competitive.[32]

Most mergers are analyzed prospectively based on estimates of market shares of the merging firms, however, where the merger has been consummated, a challenge can occur.[33] In either case, the ability to increase prices must be tied to the increase in market power that resulted from the merger.

In sum, even though a request for higher rates may not be sufficient to trigger antitrust liability, such a request may encourage a contracting party or the antitrust enforcement agencies to scrutinize other conduct of the provider. As noted above, when conduct increases market power or results in direct evidence of anticompetitive effects, it can raise antitrust concerns.[34]

6.4   IS IT LEGAL FOR A HOSPITAL SYSTEM TO OFFER A PACKAGE OF BUNDLED SERVICES TO A PAYER?

Whether it is legal for a hospital to offer a package of bundled services to a payer should be evaluated under two potential antitrust theories: tying and bundling. A hospital system with market power that engages in potentially predatory or exclusionary conduct by tying or bundling its hospitals

---

[29]   LePage's Inc. v. 3M, 324 F.3d 141, 152 (*quoting* Caribbean Broad. Sys., Ltd. v. Cable & Wireless PLC, 148 F.3d 1080, 1087 (D.C. Cir. 1998)); *see also,* United States v. Microsoft Corp., 253 F.3d 34, 58 (D.C. Cir. 2001).

[30]   Microsoft Corp., 253 F.3d at 59.

[31]   *See* Microsoft, 253 F.3d at 59.

[32]   F.T.C. v. H.J. Heinz Co., 246 F.3d 708, 720-21 (D.C. Cir. 2001).

[33]   *See* In the Matter of Evanston Northwestern Healthcare, Corp., Docket No. 9315.

[34]   *See* Microsoft, 253 F.3d at 59.

(or ancillary services) together for contracting purposes may risk being charged with monopolizing, or attempting to monopolize, in violation of Section 1 (illegal tying) or Section 2 (bundling) of the Sherman Act.

6.4.1   Tying

At its basic level, a *tying agreement* is an agreement between a buyer and a seller, whereby a seller conditions the sale of a good or service in one market on the buyer's agreement to buy a second good or service from the seller. "A tying arrangement is an agreement by a party to sell one product [the tying product] but only on the condition that the buyer also purchases a different (or tied) product, or at least agrees that he will not purchase that product from any other supplier."[35] Tying arrangements raise antitrust concerns if they foreclose competitors from the market for the tied service. Tying arrangements can also raise entry costs of competitors of the seller, as competitors may have to provide both the tied and the tying product to be competitive in the market. Last, tying arrangements may force consumers to buy a product from a seller from whom they otherwise would not buy.

Tying arrangements are challenged under Section 1 of the Sherman Act and may be challenged as *per se* or under the rule of reason. A tying claim may be valid if it contains *all* of the following: (1) the existence of two separate products; (2) the sale or an agreement to sell one product conditioned on the buyer's agreement to purchase a second product; (3) the seller's possession of sufficient economic power with respect to the tying product to appreciably restrain free competition in the market for the tied product; and (4) an impact on a "not insubstantial" amount of interstate commerce.[36]

Thus, the first question is whether there are two separate products; e.g., whether there are separate demands for the tying product and the tied product.[37] A tying arrangement requires two products; in proving that two products exist, there must be separate demands for the tying and tied product.[38] In *Jefferson Parish*, the issue was whether a hospital was engaging in illegal tying when it bundled anesthesiology services with hospital services. The Court held that a tying arrangement could not exist unless there was a "sufficient demand for the purchase of anesthesiological services separate from

[35]   Eastman Kodak Co. v. Image Technical Servs., 504 U.S. 451, 461 (1992).

[36]   *See e.g.,* Serv. & Training, Inc. v. Data Gen'l Corp., 963 F.2d 680, 683 (4th Cir. 1992).

[37]   *See* Jefferson Parish Hospital Dist. No. 2. v. Hyde, 466 U.S. 2, 19, 21–22 (1984); *see also* Power Test Petroleum Distribs., Inc. v. Calcu Gas, Inc., 754 F.2d 91, 96–98 (2d Cir. 1985).

[38]   *See* Jefferson Parish Hosp. Dist. No. 2. v. Hyde, 466 U.S. 2, 19, 21–22 (1984).

hospital services to identify a distinct product market in which it is efficient to offer anesthesiological services separately from hospital services." In other words, if customers would purchase the tied product from other sources if given the opportunity, then the tying and the tied products probably are separate.[39]

Additionally, a tie requires that the seller refuse to sell the tying product without the tied product (or the buyer was forced to buy the tied product). However, in certain instances, a large differential between the price offered for the package and the price offered for the separate products may be sufficient to support a tying claim. The general rule is that "where the buyer is free to take either product by itself there is no tying problem even though the seller may also offer the two items as a unit at a single price."[40]

However, ensuring that the products are separately available may not "preclude antitrust liability where a defendant has established its pricing policy in such a way that the only viable economic option is to purchase the tying and tied products in a single package."[41] For example, a court found an illegal tie where a seller sold a package of software support and hardware maintenance for $16,000 per year.[42] Customers were free to buy software support without the hardware maintenance, but the cost ranged from $80,000 to $160,000 per year. The court held that this was sufficient to support a tying claim because the "package induces all rational buyers of [the defendant's] software support to accept its hardware maintenance."[43]

---

[39] Note, however, that if a purchaser is buying a product that he otherwise would not have purchased there is no tying claim. As stated by the Supreme Court, when "a purchaser is 'forced' to buy a product he would not have otherwise bought even from another seller in the tied product market, there can be no adverse impact on competition." Jefferson Parish, 466 U.S. at 16.

[40] Jefferson Parrish, 466 U.S. at 10, n.17, *quoting* Northern Pac. R. Co. v. United States, 356 U.S. 1, 6, n.4 (1958).

[41] Ways & Means, Inc. v. IVAC Corporation, 506 F. Supp. 697, 701 (N.D. Cal. 1979).

[42] Virtual Maintenance, Inc. v. Prime Computer, Inc., 957 F.2d 1318 (6th 1992) (Virtual I), *vacated*, 506 U.S. 910 (1992), *on remand*, 995 F.2d 1324 (6th Cir. 1993) (Virtual II) *withdrawn and superseded*, 11 F.3d 660 (6th Cir. 1993) (Virtual III) (reaffirming and reinstating, in part, Virtual I), *cert. dismissed sub nom* Virtual Maintenance, Inc. v. Computervision Corp., 512 U.S. 1216 (1994).

[43] Virtual I, 957 F.2d at 1323; *see also* Virtual III, 11 F.3d at 666 ("An expert for Virtual testified that although Prime offered software support for sale separately, repurchase of software to obtain updates would cost as much as 900 percent more than if purchased in the software support/hardware maintenance package.").

The second element of an illegal tie is that the seller has market power in the market for the tying product.[44] Finally, there must also be an anticompetitive effect in the market for the tied product or service.[45]

A defense to a tying claim may be available if the seller can demonstrate that there is a legitimate business justification (other than that it allows the parties to extract higher prices from payers) for the tying arrangement.[46]

6.4.2 Bundling

The other consideration of a requirement to purchase services together is whether the bundling of services would be illegal under Section 2 of the Sherman Act as an act of monopolization or attempted monopolization.[47] Generally, bundling occurs when a seller offers a buyer a better price for the bundled product; e.g., a price available only if the buyer accepts the whole bundle.

Discounting only a package of services, but not discounting single services, is not necessarily anticompetitive. For instance, in *Doctor's Hospital of Jefferson, Inc. v. Southeast Medical Alliance, Inc.*, the Fifth Circuit held that a preferred provider organization (PPO) controlled by one hospital that only discounted a package of services (single services were available at full price) was not anticompetitive because of managed care competition.[48] "Competition among managed-care plans checks any anticompetitive effects of market power achievable from aggregating providers of hospital services. . ."[49] The court further stated that while "restricting the number of health care providers affiliated with a PPO can . . . reduce competition among them, [it can also] stimulate competition between health networks."[50]

---

[44]   466 U.S. at 17. In addition, most courts hold that the seller of the tying product must have some direct economic interest in the sale of the tied product before a violation can occur.

[45]   Suburban Propane v. Proctor Gas, Inc., 953 F.2d 780, 788 (2d Cir. 1992); Yentsch v. Texaco, Inc., 630 F.2d 46, 58 (2d Cir. 1980); 466 U.S. at 20 n. 31 ("resulting in economic harm to competition in the 'tied' market" (quoting Times-Picayune Publ' Co. v. United States, 345 U.S. 594, 613–14 (1953) and at 21 ("have foreclosed competition on the merits in a product market distinct from the market for the tying item.")).

[46]   Significantly, even if a *per se* tying violation is established, a defendant may prevail by showing a substantial business justification for the tie-in. *See, e.g.,* Mozart Co. v. Mercedes-Benz of North America, Inc., 833 F.2d 1342, 1348-51 (9th Cir. 1987).

[47]   *See e.g,* SmithKline Corp. v. Eli Lilly & Co., 575 F.2d 1056, 1065 (3d Cir. 1978) (bundled sale of antibiotics by Lilly violated Section 2 of the antitrust laws).

[48]   123 F.3d 301 (5th Cir. 1997).

[49]   *Id.* at 308.

[50]   *Id.*

In some circumstances, however, discounting only a bundle of services that a defendant produces may be anticompetitive. In *Ortho Diagnostic Systems v. Abbott Laboratories*, Ortho alleged that the excess amount of Abbott's unbundled prices for blood assay products over the package price included penalties for buying other tests from other suppliers.[51] Purchasing five assays cost $7.37 ($1.47 per unit) while purchasing three or fewer assays cost $10.02 ($2.00 per unit), an increase of 26.7 percent per unit. In reviewing whether this discounting structure gave Abbott a substantial advantage in the two blood assay products where Abbott had monopoly power, the court stated:

> this Court holds that a Section 2 plaintiff in a case like this—a case in which a monopolist (1) faces competition on only part of a complementary group of products; (2) offers the products both as a package and individually; and (3) effectively forces its competitors to absorb the differential between the bundled and unbundled prices of the product in which the monopolist has market power—must allege and prove either that (a) the monopolist has priced below its average variable cost or (b) the plaintiff is at least as efficient a producer of the competitive product as the defendant, but that the defendant's pricing makes it unprofitable for the plaintiff to continue to produce. Any other rule would entail too substantial a risk that the antitrust laws would be used to protect an inefficient competitor against price competition that would afford substantial benefits to consumers.[52]

Similarly, in *LePage's Inc. v. 3M*, the Third Circuit found that 3Ms rebate programs that were conditioned on purchases from multiple product lines violated Section 2 of the Sherman Act.[53] The court reasoned "[t]he principal anticompetitive effect of bundled rebates as offered by 3M is that when offered by a monopolist they may foreclose portions of the market to a potential competitor who does not manufacture [or provide] an equally diverse group of products and who therefore cannot make a comparable offer."[54] This holding was consistent with the Third Circuit's holding in *SmithKline Corp.*, where the Third Circuit held a bundled sale of antibiotics by Lilly violated Section 2 of the antitrust laws because Lilly linked "products on which Lilly faced no competition . . . with a competitive product."[55] Importantly, both

---

[51]   920 F. Supp. 455, 460-61 (S.D.N.Y. 1996).

[52]   *Id.* at 469–70.

[53]   324 F.3d 141 (3d Cir. 2003).

[54]   LePage's, 324 F.3d at 155.

[55]   SmithKline, 575 F.2d at 1065.

LePage's and *SmithKline* required the demonstration of market power in the relevant market prior to determining that the bundling was anticompetitive.

The Ninth Circuit rejected the approach of *Ortho* and *LePage's* in a case involving the bundling of hospital services where the hospital offered insurers discounts only if the hospital was the sole preferred provider for all hospital services. There the Ninth Circuit held that a "bundled discount [is] exclusionary or predatory for the purposes of a monopolization or attempted monopolization claim under §2 of the Sherman Act" if "after allocating the discount given by the [seller] on the entire bundle of products to the competitive product or products, the [seller] sold the competitive product or products below its average variable cost of producing them."[56] As a result, practitioners should be aware of the varied approaches currently taken by the courts in evaluating the potential anticompetitive effect of a bundled pricing arrangement for hospital services.

In sum, when a hospital is offering a package of bundled services, such conduct might be scrutinized for determination of whether the conduct reaches the level of an illegal tying arrangement or an illegal bundling arrangement. The market power of the hospital or hospital system is key, although not sufficient, for this evaluation. In some cases, the conduct may rise to a level to raise a risk of being challenged as anticompetitive although the conduct and the effects of the conduct are highly dependent on the facts and circumstances surrounding the arrangement.

---

[56] Cascade Health Sol'ns v. Peacehealth, 515 F.3d 883 (9th Cir. 2008).

7

Sharing Healthcare Price and Nonprice Information and Group Purchasing

Stephen P. Murphy, Esquire
Edwards Wildman Palmer LLP

This chapter's central theme—the sharing of information by competitors—examines some of the issues that often face healthcare providers pertaining to the exchange of price and cost information and participation in surveys. In addition, some of the issues that may arise as a result of participation in group purchasing organizations, a topic that has generated interest by the enforcement agencies and private parties, will be discussed. Fortunately, there are safety zones that apply to these issues. Finally, there will be a discussion on antitrust issues pertaining to the adoption and creation of clinical guidelines.

Exchanges of price and nonprice information can play an important, if not crucial, role in improving the competitive environment for healthcare providers and consumers alike. For these and other reasons, the courts and antitrust agencies review information exchanges under a rule of reason analysis. Nevertheless, as with any exchange of proprietary information among competitors, prophylactic measures must be used to avoid such exchanges being viewed as unlawful collusive behavior. In this respect, such exchanges, if not done properly, can become the basis for potential claims of *per se* unlawful price-fixing agreements or agreements with the effect of raising or stabilizing prices analyzed under the rule of reason. Of particular concern is that the exchange of current or future prices will lead to heightened scrutiny and potential attack. Although cost exchanges present less risk, they can still be problematic if part of a larger scheme to restrain competition. Information exchanges between competitors attract regulatory attention not because they are in and of themselves illegal, but because they can facilitate explicit or implicit collusion. If competitors exchange current and future prices, particularly if the future prices are not firm, then they can potentially influence each other's pricing decisions so that prices can be increased or stabilized. This type of activity by competitors is a *per se* violation of Section 1 of the Sherman Act. Similarly, if present or future production information is exchanged, then competitors may be able to lower or stabilize their output, which may result in having the effect of raising prices.[1] Even exchanges of "recent" prices charged or quoted has been found to have stabilized prices.[2] Exchanges of price information can be upheld under a rule of reason analysis if there is a legitimate business purpose that counters any arguable anticompetitive effect, or if it is unlikely that the exchange will have an unlawful effect on price or output.

Early case authority focused on the purpose for information exchanges.[3] The courts then shifted to the effects on competition as the divining rod for the legality of information exchanges.[4] The proliferation of information exchanges, particularly in the healthcare sector, highlighted the need for administrative guidance. The Department of Justice (DOJ) and the Federal Trade Commission (FTC) met this need by jointly issuing the *Statements of Antitrust Enforcement Policy in Health Care* (*Statements*) in August 1996. The *Statements* provide guidance for a variety of activities in the healthcare sector including exchanges of price and cost information.[5]

7.1 PROVIDERS ARE ASKED TO PARTICIPATE IN A PRICING INFORMATION SURVEY. ARE THEY PERMITTED TO PARTICIPATE?

Healthcare providers are permitted to participate in surveys of pricing information subject to certain limitations. The *Statements* provide a safe harbor for participation in surveys of prices for healthcare services or surveys of wages, salaries, or benefits for employees by competing providers, absent extraordinary circumstances. Entitlement to the safe harbor requires compliance with the following conditions:

- The survey is conducted by a third party like a trade association, healthcare consultant, or an academic;

---

[1]   United States v. Andreas, 216 F.3d 645, 666-69 (7th Cir. 2000).

[2]   *See* United States v. Container Corp. of America, 393 U.S. 333, 337 (1969).

[3]   *See, e.g.,* Maple Flooring Manufacturers Ass'n v. United States, 268 U.S. 563, 567 (1925).

[4]   United States v. Container Corp. of America, 393 U.S. at 344-45.

[5]   *See, e.g.,* Letter to Mit Spears, Esq from Christine Varney, Apr. 26, 2010 (exchange of price survey information would not harm competition), *available at* http://www.justice.gov/atr/public/busreview/258013.htm.

- The data provided in the survey, if it is shared with other data providers, must be at least 3 months old, but current information can be provided to customers; and
- Where information is shared with providers, at least five providers must have submitted information to the exchange, no individual provider's data can constitute 25 percent or more of that information, and any information distributed is on a sufficiently aggregated basis to foreclose identification of individual participants.[6]

These conditions are necessary to prevent competing healthcare providers from using the information exchange to collude on price or cost. Of note, the safe harbor applies only to data that is at least three months old as it specifically excludes the exchange of future prices of provider services or staff compensation. The reason why the survey must be conducted by a disinterested third party is so competitively sensitive information can be aggregated, the parties cannot see the detailed information of other parties, and to prevent any challenge that a competitor is taking advantage of access to the information for their own competitive gain. The age of the data is deemed important so as to avoid giving competitors current price trends that can lead to future price fixing. The number of data providers and the data aggregation requirement are intended to avoid identification of a specific company's prices and costs.

For those exchanges that fall outside the safe harbor, the *Statements* provide that the antitrust authorities will engage in a case-by-case weighing of anticompetitive effects as measured against the procompetitive justifications for the exchange (a classic rule of reason evaluation process). Here, in predicting the exchange's effect on competition, the agencies will review the nature of the information provided, its age, its specificity, the percentage of competitors participating in the exchange, the communications among providers concerning the information, the rationale for the exchange, and the market's structure to perform this weighing exercise—e.g., the level of market concentration. So, even if a survey or exchange falls outside of the safe harbor, if it has procompetitive effects for consumers, it can withstand antitrust scrutiny. For example, even if the information provided is current, if distribution of the survey is delayed for three months, then the same result as the *Statements* contemplate can be accomplished.[7] Or, if more than 25 percent of the information comes from one provider or fewer than five providers submit information, then the survey can still be permissible if no participant gets access to raw data,

---

[6] *See Statements* at Chap. 5, p. 25, *available at* www.justice.gov/atr/public/guidelines/0000.htm.

[7] *See* Department of Justice Business Review Letter to Brian M. Foley, at 3 (Feb. 18, 1994), *available at* http://www.justice.gov/atr/public/busreview/0783.htm.

and the survey result is so aggregated as to foreclose "reverse engineering" of provider sources.[8]

In sum, if the conditions of the *Statements* safe harbor are met or nearly so, then participation in the survey of pricing information should be permissible under the antitrust laws.

7.2 MAY HOSPITALS SHARE NONPRICE INFORMATION WITH EACH OTHER?

Typically, sharing of nonprice information does not present the type of antitrust issues that price information exchanges present, unless such information includes highly-sensitive business planning information such as strategic planning documents. Although of a less problematic nature, many of the same issues and limitations that apply to price information apply to such things as exchanges of cost information, particularly if it involves the exchange of wage and benefit information. This concern can be particularly grave if the exchange is part of a scheme to fix or manipulate prices.

The *Statements* safe harbor applies to both "price for healthcare services" as well as "wages, salaries, or benefits of healthcare personnel." Although less likely to result in naked price fixing, parties should still exercise due care concerning compliance with the safe harbor requirements when exchanging nonprice information. Hence, it is prudent to apply the same constraints noted above with respect to price information exchanges in the healthcare context when exchanging nonprice information. Even though cost exchanges do not present the same price-fixing risk as does the exchange of price information, it can present risks of output manipulation that can have an indirect impact on price.

However, no exchanges should be discussed, agreed to, or implemented without consultation with counsel. This is an area of antitrust fraught with risk, and due care needs to be exercised prior to moving forward on any such project.

7.3 MAY WAGE SURVEYS BE USED TO ASSIST IN PAYING COMPETITIVE SALARIES?

Many hospitals benchmark wages, especially nursing staff wages, to remain competitive in the market and to attract experienced caregivers. Thus, it is not unusual for a hospital to engage in salary or cost information exchanges to benchmark how the hospital is performing. *Benchmarking*

---

[8] *See* Department of Justice Business Review Letter to Mit Spears, at 7–8 (Apr. 26, 2010), *available at* http://www.justice.gov/atr/public/busreview/258013.htm.

involves a comparative analysis of cost, salary, and other data from similarly situated competitors to measure whether the collecting company's cost and salary structure meets the standards of the industry. As such, it facilitates a number of procompetitive effects and is generally permissible.

Proposals for the exchange of wage information, however, deserve particular attention because such surveys can lead to wage adjustments, and the disaffected employees may initiate litigation. In this regard, lawsuits were filed in the last few years alleging that hospitals conspired to violate Section 1 of the Sherman Antitrust Act by conspiring to suppress nurses' wages. In *Reed v. Advocate Health Care*,[9] the district court denied a motion for certification of a nurse class. The court held that if the exchange of staff registered nurses' wages was part of a conspiracy to fix such wages then it was *per se* unlawful, but in this case mere sharing of the information would be subject to a rule of reason analysis.

In *Clarke, et al. v. Baptist Memorial Healthcare Corp., et al.*,[10] the district court denied a motion to dismiss a complaint brought by registered nurses in Memphis that two hospitals had violated Section 1 by exchanging wage information. A later decision by the court denied a motion for class certification. In *Cason-Merenda, et al. v. DMC, et al.*,[11] another registered nurses class action charged eight Detroit hospitals or health systems with suppressing nurse wages through, in part, wage information exchanges. Three significant defendants entered into settlements with the plaintiffs, and these settlements were approved by the court in March 2010. Finally, in *Maderazo, et al. v. VHS San Antonio Partners L.P., et al.*,[12] local registered nurses charged three San Antonio health systems with wage suppression through wage information exchanges. The case is stayed pending the court's decision on class certification motions.

In *Jung v. Association of American Medical Colleges*,[13] the practice of exchanging medical residents' salaries among institutions with residence programs was sufficient to state a course of action under the Sherman Act. So, although nonprice exchanges are generally less problematic than price exchanges, wage and salary information exchanges will tend to be closely scrutinized. In *In re Compensation of Managerial, Professional & Technical Employees Antitrust Litigation*,[14] the district court utilized a rule of reason

---

[9] 2007 U.S. Dist. LEXIS 22816 (N.D. Ill. 2007).

[10] Case No. 2:06-cv-02377-MaV (W.D. Tenn.).

[11] Case No. 06-15601 (E.D. Mich.).

[12] Case No. 5:06-cv-00535 (W.D. Tex.).

[13] 300 F. Supp.2d 119 (D.D.C. 2004), *aff'd*, 184 F.Appx 9 (D.C. Cir. 2006), *cert. denied*, 549 U.S. 1156 (2007).

[14] 2008 U.S. Dist. LEXIS 63633 (D.N.J. 2008).

analysis to grant summary judgment to defendant employers who exchanged wage and salary information. On July 22, 2010, a federal district judge in *Fleishman v. Albany Medical Center* denied a summary judgment motion by competing upstate New York hospitals that had been charged with nurse wage fixing through a wage information exchange.[15] There, the court found that evidence of suppressed wages and underutilization of nurses was sufficient to defeat summary judgment by showing actual adverse effects.

In utilizing wage surveys, the same safe harbor standards of the *Statements* provide guidance for benchmarking efforts. Nevertheless, extreme care needs to be exercised because the whole purpose of benchmarking is to determine what local standards are and whether such standards are being met. This drive to measure relative performance can often be construed as an agreement with the company's competitors to enforce salary uniformity.

7.4 MAY A HOSPITAL ENTER INTO GROUP PURCHASING ARRANGEMENTS?

Group purchasing arrangements are extremely popular with hospitals that seek to reduce costs. Such arrangements through healthcare group purchasing organizations (GPOs) are not unlawful and often can have significant procompetitive effects,[16] such as more efficient distribution, centralized ordering, and combined warehousing. Nevertheless, the competitive risk of such arrangements is that the "group" can acquire *monopsony* (i.e., a buyer's monopoly) power. This risk is manifested when the group can manipulate the price of goods purchased, standardize costs, and permit more accurate projections of competitors' production output (through knowledge of input costs).

These risks must be accounted for while considering entering into a joint purchasing agreement. For example, in *United States v. Arizona Hospital and Healthcare Association and AZ HHA Service Corp.*,[17] an Arizona group purchasing organization contracted with nursing agencies to provide per diem and travel nurses to participating member hospitals. The DOJ sued the service corporation, as well as its parent statewide nonprofit hospital association, alleging that the joint purchasing arrangement allowed the member hospitals (through the association) to set the billing rates for the nursing agencies. These rates were allegedly below the rates the member hospitals could otherwise have achieved through independent negotiation. The defendants entered into

---

[15] CV 1:06-CV-00765 (N.D.N.Y. July 22, 2010) (McAvoy, J.).

[16] *See* Department of Justice & Federal Trade Commission, *Antitrust Guidelines for Collaborations Among Competitors* (2000) at § 3.31(a), *available at* www.justice.gov/atr/foiaroom.html.

[17] No. CV07-1030-PHX (D. Ariz. May 22, 2007).

a consent decree to resolve the charges and agreed to discontinue the pricing practices.[18]

The *Statements* note that monopsony concerns can be manifested where (1) the GPO accounts for so large a percentage of the purchasers of a given good or service that it can control price; or (2) where the percentage of the goods or services purchased are so large so as to facilitate price fixing.

Statement 7 of the *Statements* provides a safe harbor for GPOs. If (1) the GPO's purchases account for less than 35 percent of the total sales of the purchased goods or services in the relevant market; and (2) the GPO's cost of goods accounts for less than 20 percent of the total revenues from all goods and services sold by *each* member of the GPO, then the enforcement agencies (absent extraordinary circumstances) generally will not challenge the GPO arrangement.

Even if the GPO's activities fall outside this safe harbor, the conduct is not necessarily unlawful. The federal antitrust agencies and courts will utilize a case-by-case rule of reason analysis to review the purpose and effects of the individual GPO's buying practices.

7.5   ARE LOCAL HOSPITALS PERMITTED TO COLLABORATE TO DEVELOP CLINICAL PRACTICE GUIDELINES? WHAT PRECAUTIONS DO THE HOSPITALS NEED TO TAKE?

The short answer is that competitors are allowed, and in many cases, expected to collaborate regarding best practices and development of procedures to improve patient quality of care. Development and adoption of clinical guidelines or evidence-based medicine has been spurred by recent healthcare legislation and, in this regard, may require additional attention. Development of evidence-based medicine guidelines is a form of standard setting that is no different in many respects from other forms of standard setting in technology-based industries. In most instances, standard setting is procompetitive, and it results in increased quality and product functionality. Nevertheless, the antitrust laws will police standards that have the potential for anticompetitive effects in the market by, for example, excluding competitors from the market for no valid reason. In most cases, the antitrust laws will not be implicated unless there is sufficient market power, and the standard has been manipulated by participants in the standard-setting process who have an economic

---

[18]   Proposed Final Judgment, United States v. Ariz. Hosp. & Healthcare Ass'n and Az HHA Serv. Corp., No. CV07-1030-PHX (D. Ariz. May, 2007), *available at* www.usdoj.gov/atr/cases/f225800/225837.htlp://htm.

interest in the standard that is being promulgated. Furthermore, standards can be used by competitors to agree on areas where they might normally compete with one another, thereby suppressing vigorous competition.

Two antitrust issues flow from the situation where competitors set out to establish standards for clinical practice. The first issue relates to the ability of a standard-setting participant (in this case, a healthcare provider) to inappropriately influence the standard in ways that exclude their competitors from the market. The Supreme Court in *Hydrolevel v. American Society of Mechanical Engineers, Inc.*[19] suggests that a Sherman Act Section 1 violation can arise from a competitor's abuse of a standard-setting process to preclude a new market entrant. Moreover, industry standard setting has on occasion led to complaints of concerted refusals to deal. Under this theory, a competitor can join together with other companies in the standard-setting process (not necessarily competitors) to use standards to block new entrants or to eliminate existing competitors.

In the context of hospitals collaborating on clinical practice guidelines, physicians who lose privileges for failure to meet the new guidelines or outpatient specialty groups that are unduly burdened by the guidelines may raise concerted refusal-to-deal complaints. The following characteristics must be present for clinical practice guidelines to become actionable.

7.5.1   Standards Must Be Commercial

First, the standard/guideline must be sufficiently "commercial" so as to trigger the jurisdiction of the Sherman Act. One factor that is indicative of commercial activity is whether the parties are likely to receive a direct economic benefit as a result of a reduction in competition.[20] Although not necessarily a standards case, the district court in *Jung v. Association of American Medical Colleges* addressed the issue whether activity was commercial and, therefore, subject to the jurisdiction of the antitrust laws.[21] There, medical school graduates claimed that they were required to use the residency programs of the defendants and brought a class action antitrust suit alleging that the defendants conspired under Section 1 to "displace competition in the recruitment, hiring, employment, and compensation of resident physicians, for the purpose of artificially depressing, standardizing,

---

[19]   456 U.S. 556 (1982).

[20]   *See* 1B P. Areeda & H. Hovenkamp, *Antitrust Law* ¶ 262a (3d Ed. 2006).

[21]   300 F. Supp. 2d 119 (D.D.C. 2004). Subsequently, Congress passed the Pension Funding Equity Act of 2004 that amended the antitrust laws so as to prevent antitrust prosecutions arising out of the matching program challenged by the plaintiffs. *See* 339 F. Supp. 2d 26 (D.C. 2004).

and stabilizing compensation paid to resident physicians."[22] The court found that it was an issue of fact as to whether the standards were purely academic—therefore, not subject to the antitrust laws—or whether they were sufficiently commercial in nature to trigger application of the antitrust laws. To establish commercial activity, the challenger of such standard must prove "something else or more extreme."[23] In *Jung*, allegations that the Accreditation Council for Graduate Medical Education (ACGME) standards directly limited competition in the hiring of medical residents by requiring prospective residents to contractually commit to any offers they receive through the Match Program, and the ACGME's policing of the compensation levels, constituted, at the pleading state, such "extra" conduct to make the standard commercial.

7.5.2   Conflicts of Interest and Procedural Safeguards

Second, most antitrust challenges in the standard-setting process involve a claim that one of the participants utilized the standard-setting process to aid in selection of a standard that benefited it.[24] The key in these types of cases is whether the participant sufficiently disclosed its interest in the technology so as to allow the organization to make a meaningful decision in standard selection. That is, the question becomes whether a different standard would have been selected had the interest been properly disclosed.[25]

The antitrust laws focus on the standard-setting process because neither the courts nor the agencies are equipped to review the substance of the standard and, thus, become super-standard–setting bodies. As a proxy, the focus is often on the process used to create the standard and whether it was improperly manipulated.[26] Assuming appropriate procedures were followed, clinical guideline development will not usually present serious antitrust risk unless they create anticompetitive harm.

---

[22]   300 F. Supp. 2d at 126.

[23]   *Id.* at 151.

[24]   *See* American Society of Mechanical Engineers v. Hydrolevel Corp., 456 U.S. 556 (1982) (allegations that competitor misused the standard-setting process to exclude the technology of a rival).

[25]   *See* Rambus, Inc. v. Federal Trade Commission, 522 F.3d 456 (D.C. Cir. 2008), *cert. denied*, 129 S. Ct. 1318 (2009).

[26]   *See, e.g.,* Allied Tube and Conduit Corp. v. Indian Head, Inc., 486 U.S. 492 (1988).

7.5.3   Anticompetitive Harm

Finally, an important issue is whether the standard, even if manipulated, creates anticompetitive harm. The importance here is that the antitrust laws are designed to protect the competitive process, not to protect individual competitors in that process. As such, standards can affect the competitive process if there is sufficient market power. In the medical standard process, this can occur in one of two ways.

First, the standard can be anticompetitive because, for example, it improperly excludes a class of practitioners. This was the case in *Wilk v. American Medical Association*[27] where a group of chiropractors challenged an ethical standard of the American Medical Association that prohibited allopathic physicians from associating with chiropractors. At the core of that case was a concern that the chiropractors competed with the physicians at some level. Thus, guidelines that improperly exclude one group of specialists in favor of a different group have the potential to create anticompetitive harm.

Second, clinical guidelines raise more antitrust risk if, in effect, compliance is a requirement for market participation.[28] An example here would be if a guideline were deemed to be the standard of care for a particular area such that a failure to follow the procedure could be deemed a deviation from the standard. Although such instances are currently rare, they may become more frequent as both private and public payers adopt clinical standards to determine whether payment will be made to a provider.[29] The issue is whether such guidelines, whether mandatory or not, create anticompetitive harm without sufficient procompetitive justifications.

In summary, when first considering a collaboration with competing hospitals to develop clinical practice guidelines, it is critical to prepare a written document establishing the purpose for the guidelines. Next, the collaborators should consider including nonhospital representatives in the guideline preparation process. Then a written procedural plan should be established, incorporating whatever due process rights are appropriate in the situation. Lastly, consideration should be given to establishing an appeal right for aggrieved parties. Although these steps do not foreclose antitrust complaint, they will be significant evidence in a standard-setting rule of reason analysis.

In reviewing clinical guidelines, providers, including hospitals and physicians, and payers should have an understanding of the process by which

---

[27]   895 F.2d 352 (7th Cir. 1990), *cert. denied*, 110 S. Ct. 2621 (1990).

[28]   *See* Schacher v. American Academy of Ophthalmology, 870 F.2d 397 (7th Cir. 1989).

[29]   *See* Patient Protection and Affordable Care Act, H.R. 3590, 11th Cong.,___ Pub. Law. ___ Mar. 23, 2010).

such standards were created prior to adopting or enforcing such standards. If there are sufficient conflicts that would sway the standard in favor of a group of providers, then additional caution is warranted to prevent the anticompetitive application of such standards. In general, providers should examine the following:

- Have any participants agreed on a standard to collectively set prices, allocate markets, or set some variable of the competitive process?
- Do any of the participants have a financial interest in the proposed standard such that they will benefit economically?
- If there is the potential for an economic conflict of interest, has the conflict been disclosed and were the organization's policies followed?
- If there were undisclosed conflicts of interest, do the entities have market power (i.e., the ability to control price or exclude competition) over the input or output markets?

The rule of reason will generally apply to the creation of clinical guidelines. Guidelines that are not exclusionary typically cause much less anticompetitive effect. Nevertheless, even guidelines that exclude some participants do not necessarily violate the antitrust laws if there are sufficient quality justifications for them. Entities considering such guidelines should, however, understand that there are potential anticompetitive risks when standards are used to preclude competition under the guise of improving quality.

Resources

Department of Justice and Federal Trade Commission, *Statements of Antitrust Enforcement Policy in Health Care* (August 1996), *available at* www.justice;gov/atr/public/guidelines/000.htm.

Department of Justice and Federal Trade Commission, *Antitrust Guidelines for Collaboration among Competitors* (2000), *available at* www.justice.gov/atr/foiavoom.html.

8

Litigation and Enforcement

Hillary A. Webber, Esquire

McDermott Will & Emery LLP

This chapter examines some typical procedural questions regarding discovery and enforcement in antitrust cases. It also discusses the roles of federal, state, and private parties in antitrust enforcement. Finally, it discusses the guidance that may be available to parties contemplating deals that may implicate the antitrust laws.

8.1 DO WE NEED TO COMPLY WITH A THIRD-PARTY SUBPOENA OR REQUEST FROM THE GOVERNMENT FOR DETAILED MARKET INFORMATION, INCLUDING INFORMATION IN ELECTRONIC FORM?

An individual or company should not ignore a properly served subpoena, as failure to respond to a subpoena can ultimately be punishable as contempt of court.[1] A recipient of a subpoena or other information request should consult an attorney, because a subpoena may request information, such as privileged communications, to which the requesting party is not entitled. The Federal Rules of Civil Procedure provide some protection for subpoena recipients against overly burdensome requests. Rule 45 requires a party issuing a subpoena to take reasonable steps to avoid imposing an undue burden on a subpoena recipient, and a court may impose sanctions on a party that fails to comply with this duty.[2]

The recipient of a burdensome subpoena for production of documents may respond with written objections.[3] For example, a subpoena recipient could object to a request for electronically stored information from sources that are not reasonably accessible.[4] Often, the requesting party will be willing to negotiate and narrow the scope of the subpoena and/or agree to a rolling

---

[1] Fed. R. Civ. P. 45(e).

[2] Fed. R. Civ. P. 45(c)(1).

[3] Fed. R. Civ. P. 45(c)(2)(B).

[4] Fed. R. Civ. P. 45(d)(1)(D).

production of documents to lessen the burden and cost to the recipient. If the recipient of a subpoena serves written objections, the party that served the subpoena may move the court to compel production of the requested information. On a motion to compel, the moving party bears the burden of establishing good cause for its subpoena. The court has discretion to specify conditions for discovery, such as limiting the scope of the subpoena and shifting the allocation of costs.

Another option for a recipient of a burdensome subpoena is to move the court for a protective order under Federal Rule of Civil Procedure 26(c). Any person or party from whom discovery is sought may make the motion after a good faith attempt to resolve the discovery dispute with the requesting party. The party seeking the protective order bears the burden of demonstrating good cause for the protection of the material sought. There are various types of protective orders that a court can issue, including an order precluding discovery, an order specifying the terms or method of discovery, an order limiting the scope of discovery, and an order regarding the confidentiality of disclosed information. A court has broad discretion to determine whether to grant a protective order and to determine the form of protection warranted.

In some cases, such as at the beginning of a merger investigation, an antitrust agency may issue voluntary requests for information. Although a response may be voluntary, failure to respond may trigger a subpoena for the same information. Thus, in some instances, it may be more efficient and productive to negotiate with the agency to narrow the scope of a voluntary request and produce the requested information on a voluntary basis rather than risk a subpoena.

8.2   IS THERE A STATUTE OF LIMITATIONS FOR ANTITRUST VIOLATIONS?

The Clayton Act establishes a 4-year statute of limitations for private actions.[5] The limitations period begins to run when a cause of action accrues, generally when a defendant commits an act that injures a plaintiff's business.[6] However, in the case of a continuing violation—that is, a violation that continues over time and is comprised of a series of overt acts—the statute of limitations begins to run from the last overt act that injured the plaintiff. To restart a limitations period, an overt act must be a new, independent act rather

---

[5] 15 U.S.C. § 15b.

[6] *See* Zenith Radio Corp. v. Hazeltine Research, 401 U.S. 321, 328 (1971) ("[E]ach time a plaintiff is injured by an act of the defendants a cause of action accrues to him to recover the damages caused by that act and . . . as to those damages, the statute of limitations runs from the commission of the act.").

than a reaffirmation of a previous act, and the overt act must inflict new injury on the plaintiff.[7]

Section 5(i) of the Clayton Act provides for the suspension of the limitations period for private actions during the pendency of a civil or criminal antitrust proceeding brought by the United States and for one year after, where the private action is based in whole or in part on any matter complained of in the government suit.[8] The private action must be brought within a year after the termination of the government action. When Section 5(i) applies, a plaintiff may seek damages that accrued beginning 4 years prior to the initiation of the government action. Plaintiffs most commonly use Section 5(i) to toll the limitations period following a civil or criminal action brought by the Department of Justice (DOJ) Antitrust Division, though most courts have held that antitrust proceedings brought by the Federal Trade Commission (FTC) can also trigger a suspension of the limitations period.

Fraudulent concealment of an antitrust violation also tolls the limitations period. Here, a plaintiff must establish that a defendant wrongfully concealed an antitrust offense and that the plaintiff, despite exercising reasonable diligence, did not have knowledge of the antitrust violation. Most courts have held that the statute of limitations is tolled only if the defendant engaged in "affirmative acts" of concealment.[9] In other words, absent a fiduciary relationship, mere silence is not enough to constitute fraudulent concealment. If fraudulent concealment is established, the statute of limitations begins to run when the plaintiff knew or should have known the facts that form the basis of its claim.

The United States Code provides for a five-year statute of limitations for a criminal violation of the Sherman Act.[10] In contrast to the rules for accrual of a civil conspiracy claim, in a criminal conspiracy "[a]s long as *some* part of the conspiracy continued into the five-year period preceding the indictment, the statute of limitations [does] not insulate [the defendant] from criminal liability for actions taken more than 5 years prior to the time of indictment."[11] The limitations period continues to run during an Antitrust Division investigation and the impaneling of a grand jury until a defendant is charged with a criminal antitrust offense.

---

[7]   *See* Klehr v. A.O. Smith Corp., 521 U.S. 179, 189–90 (1997).

[8]   15 U.S.C. § 16(i).

[9]   *See, e.g.*, Chapple v. National Starch & Chem. Co., 178 F.3d 501, 507 (7th Cir. 1999).

[10]   18 U.S.C. § 3282(a).

[11]   Flintkote Co. v. United States, 7 F.3d 870, 873 (9th Cir. 1993).

8.3 HOW ARE ANTITRUST LAWS ENFORCED?

The antitrust laws are enforced by federal and state government and private persons.

8.3.1 Federal Enforcement

The Antitrust Division has exclusive authority for criminal enforcement of federal antitrust laws. Criminal actions are typically brought under Section 1 of the Sherman Act, which prohibits certain contracts, combinations, and conspiracies that unreasonably restrain trade. Criminal enforcement has traditionally been reserved for the most pernicious antitrust violations, which are considered *per se* illegal, such as horizontal price-fixing conspiracies, bid-rigging, and market or customer allocation.

On the civil side, both the Antitrust Division and the FTC enforce the federal antitrust laws. The Antitrust Division has exclusive authority to enforce the Sherman Act on behalf of the federal government, and it shares authority with the FTC and other agencies to enforce the Clayton Act.

The FTC is an independent agency with exclusive jurisdiction to administer the FTC Act, which prohibits unfair methods of competition and unfair or deceptive acts or practices.[12] The FTC's jurisdiction under the FTC Act covers a broad range of conduct, including any conduct prohibited by the antitrust statutes. Thus, although the FTC cannot directly enforce the Sherman Act, the FTC can prosecute violations of the Sherman Act as an unfair method of competition under the FTC Act.[13] The FTC can enforce the Clayton Act and the Robinson-Patman Act directly or as unfair methods of competition under the FTC Act.

To ensure that both agencies do not investigate the same matter, matters are assigned to one agency or the other based on a clearance procedure. Often, clearance is readily granted to either the Antitrust Division or the FTC, but in some cases the agencies petition one another for clearance. In general, each agency has established areas of expertise and handles matters arising in those areas. For instance, the Antitrust Division has historically handled enforcement matters relating to healthcare insurers, while the FTC has focused on health care providers.

---

[12]   15 U.S.C. § 45.

[13]   *See, e.g.*, FTC v. Motion Picture Adver. Serv., 344 U.S. 392, 394–95 (1953).

8.3.2   State Enforcement

State attorneys general may also enforce the antitrust laws and frequently coordinate with federal authorities and other states in antitrust investigations and lawsuits. Almost all states and the District of Columbia have some form of antitrust statute, typically modeled after the federal antitrust laws (*see* Appendix A for a listing of principal state antitrust provisions). Most state attorneys general may bring a state antitrust action for damages on behalf of the state, its agencies, and political subdivisions as purchasers of goods or services.[14] In addition, many state statutes provide for *parens patriae* actions on behalf of residents.[15] Most state statutes provide for criminal penalties for violations of the state's antitrust laws. These penalties tend to be less severe than their federal counterparts.

State attorneys general may also file federal antitrust actions on behalf of the state as a purchaser. A state, as well as cities and political subdivisions, qualifies as a "person" for purposes of the Clayton Act, so a state attorney general may sue in its proprietary capacity as a direct purchaser of goods and services and may collect treble damages for injury sustained as a result of an antitrust violation. A state is not permitted to recover damages for injury to its general economy because such recovery could be duplicative of individual persons' recovery.

A state can sue for injunctive relief under Section 16 of the Clayton Act when a violation of the antitrust laws threatens harm to the state.[16] Unlike state-initiated damages actions, a state may seek injunctive relief based on the threat of injury to the state's general economy.

The Clayton Act further provides that a state attorney general may bring a federal treble damages action as *parens patriae* on behalf of the natural persons residing in the state.[17] This *parens patriae* authority is limited to damages arising from violations of the Sherman Act and to damages sought on behalf of direct purchasers. *Parens patriae* actions are distinct from class actions and do not require certification to proceed.

8.3.3   Private Enforcement

Under Section 4 of the Clayton Act, private parties may seek treble damages for violations of the federal antitrust laws.[18] To sue for damages,

---

[14]   *See, e.g.*, Ariz. Rev. Stat. § 44-1408; Cal. Bus. & Prof. Code § 16570.

[15]   *See, e.g.*, Alaska Stat. § 45.50.577; Conn. Gen. Stat. § 35-32(c).

[16]   15 U.S.C. § 26.

[17]   15 U.S.C. § 15c(a)(1).

[18]   15 U.S.C. § 15(a).

a private plaintiff must establish standing by demonstrating: (1) that it has suffered injury-in-fact to its business or property, (2) that the injury constitutes "antitrust injury," and (3) that the injury is not too remote from the alleged violation.

To satisfy the first element—injury-in-fact—a plaintiff must show that the defendant's conduct caused injury to the plaintiff's business or property. The conduct does not need to be the sole cause of injury, but it must be a substantial and material cause of the plaintiff's injury. The second element—antitrust injury—is "injury of the type the antitrust laws were intended to prevent and that flows from that which makes the defendant's acts unlawful."[19] In other words, a plaintiff must demonstrate that the injury is of the type that causes harm to competition, not merely to the plaintiff. If the plaintiff's injury is the result of procompetitive conduct, a court will refuse to find standing. Third, a plaintiff must establish that its injury is not too far removed from the violation or, stated differently, that other parties are not better situated to bring suit. In evaluating remoteness, courts look to factors including the causal connection between the conduct and the injury, the nature and directness of the injury (e.g., whether the plaintiff is a consumer or competitor in the relevant market), the potential for duplicative recovery, and the existence of more direct victims.[20]

In the case of injunctive relief, the standing requirements are slightly different. A plaintiff seeking an injunction need show only threatened injury from an impending violation of the antitrust laws rather than actual injury.[21]

The Supreme Court has ruled that an indirect purchaser—a consumer that does not purchase directly from a defendant but rather through an innocent intermediary—does not have standing to recover damages under the federal antitrust laws, except in certain rare circumstances. The rationale behind this doctrine, known as the *Illinois Brick*[22] rule, is that permitting both indirect and direct purchasers to recover damages for the same conduct would be duplicative and that apportioning damages among levels of purchasers would be too complex and burdensome. An indirect purchaser may, however, pursue an injunction under the federal antitrust laws, as a suit in equity does not implicate the same concerns of duplicative and complex apportionment of damages.

Private parties can also bring actions under state antitrust laws. Most state antitrust laws, like their federal counterparts, provide for treble damages and

---

[19] Atlantic Richfield Co. v. USA Petroleum Co., 495 U.S. 328, 334 (1990).

[20] *See* Associated General Contractors v. California State Council of Carpenters, 459 U.S. 519 (1983).

[21] 15 U.S.C. § 26.

[22] *See* Illinois Brick Co. v. Illinois, 431 U.S. 720 (1977).

injunctive relief. In fact, state antitrust remedies are often more comprehensive than federal antitrust remedies, making state antitrust enforcement an attractive option for private plaintiffs. For example, a number of states have legislatively repealed the bar to indirect purchaser damages established in *Illinois Brick* and permit a cause of action for indirect purchasers under state law.[23]

8.4 WHAT AUTHORITY DO STATE ATTORNEYS GENERAL HAVE TO INVESTIGATE FEDERAL ANTITRUST VIOLATIONS?

State antitrust statutes generally provide state attorneys general with broad authority to investigate antitrust violations. This investigative authority typically includes the power to issue subpoenas and interrogatories and to compel testimony. Some state statutes specifically grant the state attorney general authority to investigate suspected antitrust violations under federal law.[24] Other state antitrust statutes confer authority on the state attorney general to investigate potential antitrust violations generally or violations of the state antitrust statute.[25] As discussed above, state antitrust statutes are generally modeled after federal antitrust law, and state attorneys general may bring federal antitrust claims. In practice, therefore, an investigation into potential violations of state antitrust law could lead to a federal antitrust lawsuit.

Cooperation among state and federal authorities in antitrust investigations occurs frequently. The Clayton Act provides that a state attorney general may request from the Attorney General of the United States any investigative files or other materials that may be relevant to a cause of action under the Clayton Act.[26]

8.5 WHAT DAMAGES ARE AVAILABLE TO PLAINTIFFS IN PRIVATE ANTITRUST LAWSUITS?

Section 4(a) of the Clayton Act provides that private parties are entitled to treble damages and the cost of suit including reasonable attorneys' fees for violations of federal antitrust law.[27] The automatic trebling of a damages

---

[23] *See, e.g.*, Cal. Bus. & Prof. Code § 16750(a); 740 Ill. Comp. Stat. Ann. 10/7(2); N.Y. Gen. Bus. Law § 340(6).

[24] *See, e.g.*, Fla. Stat. § 542.27(3); Colo. Rev. Stat. § 6-4-111.

[25] *See, e.g.*, Cal Gov't Code § 1180; Conn. Gen. Stat. § 35-42; 740 Ill. Comp. Stat. § 10/7.2.

[26] 15 U.S.C. § 15f(b).

[27] 15 U.S.C. § 15(a).

award in private antitrust actions is intended to promote private enforcement of the antitrust laws and to deter potential and repeated offenders. The measure of damages is case-specific, but, in general, a successful antitrust plaintiff can recover lost profits, overcharges, and loss of going concern value.

In antitrust conspiracy cases, a potential damages award can be especially high because a defendant is joint and severally liable for the damages caused by each co-conspirator, with no right of contribution. Thus, a single defendant in an antitrust price-fixing conspiracy can be liable for three times the damages attributable to overcharges paid by all customers in the market, not only the defendant's own customers.

Under Section 4 of the Clayton Act, prevailing plaintiffs (or counterclaimants) may recover reasonable attorneys' fees and costs. An award of attorneys' fees to a successful plaintiff is mandatory, even if the damage award is nominal. Recovery of other costs of suit is subject to the court's discretion. Attorneys' fees and other costs of suit are similarly available to a plaintiff who substantially prevails in an injunctive suit.[28] With limited exceptions, a successful antitrust defendant may not recover attorneys' fees.

8.6 HOW DO WE MAKE A COMPLAINT TO THE GOVERNMENTAL AGENCIES REGARDING A COMPETITOR'S POTENTIAL ANTICOMPETITIVE PRACTICE?

Most government antitrust authorities provide information on their Web sites about filing a complaint regarding anticompetitive conduct. For example, a person may file a complaint with the FTC through its online complaint form.[29] Alternatively, the FTC's "Contact Us" Web page provides telephone number and mailing address information, through which a concerned party can make a complaint.[30] Similarly, the Antitrust Division provides information on its Web site for submitting an antitrust-related complaint by e-mail, regular mail, or phone.[31] Most states' attorney general Web sites likewise provide information for filing a complaint.

---

[28] 15 U.S.C. § 26.

[29] FTC, Complaint Assistant, *available at* https://www.ftccomplaintassistant.gov/.

[30] FTC, Contact Us, *available at* http://www.ftc.gov/ftc/contact.shtm.

[31] U.S. Department of Justice, Reporting Antitrust Concerns, *available at* http://www.justice.gov/atr/contact/newcase.html.

8.7 WHAT TYPE OF ANTITRUST GUIDANCE IS AVAILABLE FROM THE GOVERNMENT?

Government Web sites are an excellent source of information about the antitrust laws and enforcement activities.

For general antitrust background, the *FTC Guide to the Antitrust Laws* is available through the FTC's Web site.[32] The *Guide* provides an overview of the antitrust laws and enforcers, guidance on dealing with competitors and the supply chain, and information on anticompetitive single-firm conduct and merger review.

Similarly, the Antitrust Division offers an array of antitrust guidance materials on its Web site,[33] including an overview of statutes relevant to the Antitrust Division[34] and a summary of the recently revised merger guidelines.[35]

For guidance focused on healthcare antitrust, *Statements of Antitrust Enforcement Policy in Health Care*, issued by the FTC and Antitrust Division together, is a useful resource.[36] The *Statements* resource provides guidance as to how the agencies evaluate antitrust issues in healthcare contexts—such as provider network formation—and offers examples and analyses to illustrate enforcement principles. FTC and Antitrust Division guidance on the formation of accountable care organizations is likewise available online.[37]

In addition, for parties contemplating transactions that may implicate the antitrust laws, both the FTC and Antitrust Division offer an advisory opinion/business review process.[38] An advisory opinion or business review is an agency's statement of its current enforcement intentions with respect to proposed business conduct. The request for an advisory opinion must be made before engaging in the activity for which the party is requesting the opinion.

---

[32] FTC, Guide to the Antitrust Laws, *available at* http://www.ftc.gov/bc/antitrust/index.shtm.

[33] Department of Justice: Antitrust Division, Business Resources, *available at* http://www.justice.gov/atr/public/business-resources.html.

[34] Department of Justice: Antitrust Division, Division Manual, *available at* http://www.justice.gov/atr/public/divisionmanual/chapter2.pdf.

[35] FTC and Antitrust Division, Horizontal Merger Guidelines, *available at* http://www.justice.gov/atr/public/guidelines/hmg-2010.html.

[36] FTC and Antitrust Division, Statements of Antitrust Enforcement Policy in Healthcare, *available at* http://www.justice.gov/atr/public/guidelines/1791.htm.

[37] FTC and Antitrust Division, Statement of Antitrust Enforcement Policy Regarding Accountable Care Organizations Participating in the Medicare Shared Savings Program, *available at* http://www.ftc.gov/os/fedreg/2011/10/111020aco.pdf.

[38] The FTC Advisory opinion process is set forth in 16 C.F.R. §§ 1.1-1.4, and the DOJ Business Review Process is set forth in 28 CFR § 50.6.

Furthermore, there must be a commitment to enter into the transaction if the matter is reviewed favorably. In this regard, a proposed course of action must be sufficiently developed for the agencies to conclude that it is an actual proposal, not a mere possibility.

The FTC advisory opinion process specifically prohibits an advisory opinion where: (1) the same or substantially the same course of action is under investigation; (2) the same or essentially the same course of action is or has been the subject of a current proceeding involving the Commission or another governmental agency; or (3) an informed opinion cannot be made or could be made only after extensive investigation, clinical study, testing, or collateral inquiry.

In most situations in healthcare, the opinion or review letter will state whether the agencies would consider a matter *per se* unlawful or would evaluate the proposed conduct under the rule of reason. It is frequently impossible for the agencies to determine the exact anticompetitive effects of proposed conduct without a full market analysis, which they will not undertake. Thus, unless the activity falls under one of the safe harbors (for example, certain hospital mergers or development of certain accountable care organizations), the agencies will not issue an opinion stating that the conduct will be immune from antitrust challenge. Instead, the opinion/review will likely say only that the conduct would be analyzed under the rule of reason. With regard to network contracting issues, this may be an important concession, as it will allow the proposed network to argue that the procompetitive justifications outweigh any anticompetitive harm.

A collection of advisory opinions and business reviews may be found on the FTC and Antitrust Division Web sites, respectively.[39]

---

[39] FTC, Advisory Opinions (Healthcare), *available at* http://www.ftc.gov/bc/healthcare/industryguide/advisory.htm; Department of Justice: Antitrust Division, Business Review Letters, *available at* http://www.justice.gov/atr/public/busreview/index.html.

Appendix A

State Antitrust Laws

State	Principal Antitrust Provisions
Alabama	Ala. Code § 8-10-1 *et seq.*
Alaska	Alaska Stat. § 45.50.562 *et seq.*
Arizona	Ariz. Rev. Stat. Ann. § 44-1401 *et seq.*
Arkansas	Ark. Const. art. 2, § 19; Ark. Stat. Ann. § 4-75-301 *et seq.*
California	Cal. Bus. & Prof. Code § 16700 *et seq.*
Colorado	Colo. Rev. Stat. § 6-4-101 *et seq.*
Connecticut	Conn. Gen. Stat. § 35-26 *et seq.*
Delaware	Del. Code Ann. tit. 6, § 2101 *et seq.*
District of Columbia	15 U.S.C. § 3; D.C. Code § 28-4501 *et seq.*
Florida	Fla. Stat. § 542.15 *et seq.*
Georgia	Ga. Code Ann. § 13-8-2; Ga. Const. art. III, § 6, P 5(c).
Hawaii	Haw. Rev. Stat. § 480-1 *et seq.*
Idaho	Idaho Code Ann. § 48-101 *et seq.*
Illinois	740 Ill. Comp. Stat. § 10/1 *et seq.*
Indiana	Ind. Code Ann. § 24-1-1-1 *et seq.*
Iowa	Iowa Code § 553.1 *et seq.*
Kansas	Kan. Stat. Ann. § 50-101 *et seq.*
Kentucky	Ky. Rev. Stat. Ann. § 367.170 *et seq.*
Louisiana	La. Rev. Stat. Ann. § 51:121 *et seq.*
Maine	Me. Rev. Stat. Ann. tit. 10, § 1101 *et seq.*
Maryland	Md. Code Ann. § 11-201 *et seq.*
Massachusetts	Mass. Gen. Laws Ann. ch. 93, § 1 *et seq.*
Michigan	Mich. Comp. Laws Ann. § 445.771 *et seq.*

State	Principal Antitrust Provisions
Minnesota	Minn. Stat. § 325D.49 *et seq.*
Mississippi	Miss. Code Ann. § 75-21-1 *et seq.*
Missouri	Mo. Rev. Stat. § 416.011 *et seq.*
Montana	Mont. Code Ann. § 30-14-201 *et seq.*
Nebraska	Neb. Rev. Stat. § 59-801 *et seq.*
Nevada	Nev. Rev. Stat. § 598A.010 *et seq.*
New Hampshire	N.H. Rev. Stat. Ann. § 356:1 *et seq.*
New Jersey	N.J. Stat. Ann. § 56:9-1 *et seq.*
New Mexico	N.M. Stat. Ann. § 57-1-1 *et seq.*
New York	N.Y. Gen. Bus. Law § 340 *et seq.*
North Carolina	N.C. Gen. Stat. § 75-1 *et seq.*
North Dakota	N.D. Cent. Code § 51-08.1-01 *et seq.*
Ohio	Ohio Rev. Code § 1331.01 *et seq.*
Oklahoma	Okla. Stat. tit. 79, § 201 *et seq.*
Oregon	Or. Rev. Stat. § 646.705 *et seq.*
Pennsylvania	No antitrust statute of general application. The state relies on common law restraint of trade and monopoly doctrine.
Rhode Island	R.I. Gen. Laws § 6-36-1 *et seq.*
South Carolina	S.C. Code Ann. § 39-3-10 *et seq.*
South Dakota	S.D. Codified Laws Ann. § 37-1-3.1 *et seq.*
Tennessee	Tenn. Code Ann. § 47-25-101 *et seq.*
Texas	Tex. Bus. & Com. Code Ann. § 15.01 *et seq.*
Utah	Utah Code Ann. § 76-10-911 *et seq.*
Vermont	No antitrust statute of general application. The state relies on common law restraint of trade and monopoly doctrine.
Virginia	Va. Code Ann. § 59.1-9.1 *et seq.*

State	Principal Antitrust Provisions
Washington	Wash. Rev. Code Ann. § 19.86.010 *et seq.*
West Virginia	W. Va. Code § 47-18-1 *et seq.*
Wisconsin	Wis. Stat. Ann. § 133.01 *et seq.*
Wyoming	Wyo. Stat. Ann. § 40-4-101 *et seq.*; Wyo. Const. Art. 1, § 30; Art. 10, § 8.

Index